Sheep
for all
Seasons

Praise for Sue Andrews:

"An enchanting picture of farming life, full of warmth and humour" - Katie Fforde

"An engaging and immersive read ... the reader soon realises that farming is a way of life rather than a job"

"Informative and enjoyable"

"Loved this and so well written you could just be there"

"Oh how I enjoyed this book! ... A good and amusing read for everyone, not just sheep afficionados. It has thoroughly re-kindled my desire to keep sheep and I shall be looking for a couple of elderly in-lamb ewes this Autumn. Thank you, Sue Andrews!!"

"Opening this book is like stepping into the countryside. I loved it. I love sheep and now I love them even more. I highly recommend this beautiful book"

"Brilliant read and full of country humour"

Sue Andrews

Sheep for all Seasons

A year of lambs, sheepdogs and new
adventures on the farm

Crumps Barn Studio

Crumps Barn Studio
Crumps Barn, Syde, Cheltenham GL53 9PN
www.crumpsbarnstudio.co.uk

Cover images: Clouds © Tampatra1 / Dreamstime.com | Sue Andrews | Lorna Gray | Ian Street
Design by Lorna Gray © Crumps Barn Studio
Photographic plates © Sue Andrews | Lorna Gray | Ian Street | Alfie Shaw

Printed in Gloucestershire on FSC certified paper by Severn, a carbon neutral company

ISBN 978-1-915067-01-2

To my husband, with all my love.
This is a year we've spent very much
together and thoroughly enjoyed

AN INTRODUCTION

We farm at Sudgrove, just outside Miserden, on the Cotswold escarpment looking down towards the River Severn. Not isolated, but in an area where we hear birdsong, wildlife and agricultural machines rather than general traffic. This is despite the fact we are only nine miles from the city of Gloucester. We also rent land at Edgeworth and our son Mark has recently purchased the adjacent hundred acres now called Bisley Lane Farm, although we often still refer to it as Red Sheds, as it was previously known! Mind you, I still refer to Pink Cottages, which have been demolished for over thirty years and replaced by Bisley Lane House. Obviously an age thing.

We run about 110 Texel ewes, 50 Blue Texels and

a small flock of Lleyn x Texel commercials, although I keep suggesting we cut down a bit. Our horses are now reduced to a cantankerous old pony, Clemmie.

We first took over the farm at Sudgrove some thirty years ago. In those days, we only had 40 acres of grass banks – the cost of renting the flat top fields that were growing wheat and barley was beyond us. We were so envious of the enormous livestock building where the contractor who rented the arable acres was storing his straw, particularly on those cold spring mornings when lambing began in our far less palatial sheds …

As time went on our landlady, the famous showjumper Pat Smythe, suggested she would like just one tenant, so finances were carefully calculated, discussions were held with the bank manager and with trepidation we dared to rent the whole 110 acres and that wonderful, enormous animal barn. What a dream that was!

I'm still today, some twenty years into that relationship, blocking up gaps between the wooden sleepers along the base of the barn and the metal sides with wads of straw, stopping lambs from falling into the gaps made by the contractor's big hay and straw bales when they were pushed too hard against the outer walls.

But it is good to have it back fulfilling the purpose it was originally built for, even if it does face west, where most of the prevailing wind and rain comes from.

Behind this main sheep shed we have a number of other buildings, with names that tell their own story. The Black Shed has some black plastic boards across part of the front, the Bike Shed is where the quads are kept and the stables are self-explanatory. The New Shed was our own construction some ten years ago, replacing a polytunnel that survived our hilltop weather for over twenty years. The New Shed merges with the Grain Store where the drier was housed in arable days, but which now provides accommodation for lambing pens and feedstuffs in ton totes, then extends behind the New Shed to house the hay. All in all, we're extremely well off for buildings.

Home is about a quarter of a mile away. We've lived in this farmhouse for over thirty years. Named Lypiatt Farm, it was originally tied in with Aubrey's job as Arable Foreman on the neighbouring estate and before that it was both a house and dairy. Built in the silvery grey weathered Cotswold stone, it is warm in winter and cool in summer. The garden – not particularly well looked after, although it does look quite presentable when the grass is cut – always has a cool breeze blowing through. One of my favourite hideaways is under the laburnum tree in the corner, close to the graves of my devoted dogs. Hot summer afternoons are not a time to do anything with livestock, but I can hide from view and drift into a good book.

Conveniently our land begins just behind Lypiatt Farm buildings and there is a footpath down our 9 acre field where I walk the dogs to the farm every day. The dogs enjoy their freedom and it gives me time to sort out my brain and check my body's still working. On a summer's morning, I walk through grass and wildflowers and listen to birdsong, skylarks often particularly vocal. Although we originally grew some corn, our land is now all grassland with countryside stewardship seeding, benefitting both birds and wildlife.

Everywhere is the memory of how our dream began with just a few acres. I was a horse-mad girl and Aubrey was the son of a farm manager without land or money. But we did it anyway. As our flock and our savings grew, long before finding Sudgrove, we tried to rent several of the Country Council farms that came available. I spent hours filling in applications, we walked round so called 'starter farms' and dreamed of living and working there. Sadly, there was no such thing as a 'starter farm' unless you had a very substantial amount in the bank and preferably a father who could gift you fifty heifers. There was no way a young couple with only a small amount of savings and twenty ewes were ever going to secure such a property, even with the backing of the bank. Now most of the County Councils seem to have sold off the majority of their farms, so even those from farming families wishing to branch out on their own, with family help, are struggling.

But now we're here, and farming is a way of life. It can be tiring, emotional, worrying, but there is little we'd change. We're a true team; we can argue, we can laugh together, but we're both working in the same direction. Farming life is sometimes all about leaning on a gate together on a warm summers evening, taking in the view and admiring our stock, appreciating that the hard work was all worthwhile.

This past year has been so different from most with Covid still prevalent. And for us it has brought other unexpected changes too – mainly through the addition of a young sheepdog and our son Mark turning our sheds and stables into a pig nursery on a regular basis.

We've ventured into a new breed of sheep and our stock has received high acclaim.

Mark and his wife Kate have just started rearing traditional beef cattle in their fields and Gloucester Old Spot x Pietrain pigs run around in the woods. They want to produce top quality pork, bacon and beef to sell locally, and the grandchildren relish this farming life.

So, all these years after Aub and I first set out to follow our own farming dream, we hope we can help them find their feet.

With Aub, Maisie and some of the lambs

AUGUST

It's mid-August, so too early to count as autumn – the start of the farming year – but Mark's pigs don't really care about things like that. His first venture into farming is embodied by Spot and Dot, two Gloucester Old Spot sows. They have been enjoying life, playing happily in their woodland paddock at Bisley Lane, doing nothing constructive for at least eighteen months.

For some time Aub and I had emphasised to Mark that perhaps it was time these two delightful pigs did a little more than eat and grow, and produced some piglets. Fortunately, Mark is running this as a hobby, not a financially viable project. If he ever works out what these Gloucester Old Spot girls have cost him, he may realise that although a profit is not essential, a large loss is ridiculous.

I suggested borrowing a boar, as one of Aub's many

cousins had just purchased one to serve her two pigs. As usual, my ignorance of pigs was emphasised – I was told firmly that introducing a new boar could bring in disease. More to the point was Mark's desire to pair his sows with a Hungarian Mangalitser, a strange looking pig with curly hair covering it from head to tail. The piglets would have meat marbled throughout with fat – making ideal eating. His plan was to buy semen and artificially inseminate (AI) Spot and Dot, which promptly turned into the latest little adventure with which Aub became unwittingly involved ...

The only place to purchase this particular semen was Ireland, but at the time it was required the Mangalitser boar was unavailable.

The sows, Spot and Dot, actually belonged to Mark's young sons – 7 year old Wilfred owned Spot and Toby, aged 9, owned Dot. With a Mangalitser boar not in the running, the boys got to choose the parentage of the piglets, British Lop for one and Duroc for the other, and they were intending to supervise the AI process too, though Wilfred was definitely losing interest by this point – Toby is our potential farmer.

Timing was of the essence. As was practicality of management, so both sows arrived back in the stables at Sudgrove. With no boar available, the sows' receptive moments had to be judged by whether they humped their backs right up when stroked or rubbed. Being very much pet pigs, this hardly varied, as it always happened when tickled. However, the pig experts felt they knew when the time was right and semen was sent for at the set date.

Back in June we had asked our sheep scanner, who had come to backfat scan the sheep, if he was happy to try his luck scanning the sows. He agreed, although he was a little bit taken aback by the fact that at this point they were running around our back garden behind an electric fence. As Stuart, quite understandably, wasn't keen to have any of his very expensive machinery damaged, it was a case of tempting the two girls close to the fence to gauge a result on the scanner.

After considerable athletics by Aub which involved leaping the live fence a couple of times, an image showed several black dots, suggesting that Spot was carrying a number of piglets. Dot was rather shy and subsequently didn't really take part in the scanning procedure, but we all agreed, looking at her shape and the difference between the two sows' teats, it was looking less likely that Dot was actually going to give birth.

Three months, three weeks and between three and six days after conception, the day arrived when the happy event was due to take place again at Sudgrove, as we had the most suitable building for a litter of piglets. Unfortunately, it was also the day Aub and I had chosen to take our three grandsons to Crocodiles of the World. The weather recently had been poor and the mainly inside-based entertainment seemed ideal. Of course, that day the sun shone as hot as any day during the summer and I rather regretted the advanced booked tickets, but the attraction was high on the boys' list to visit – we were trying to make the most of late summer holiday activities now that lockdown restrictions had eased.

Mark and Toby were on site at Sudgrove early that morning, being responsible for daily pig management. Mark was convinced today was the day, because Spot was looking very uncomfortable. Her flanks could be seen heaving, indicating some muscular contractions, but alarmingly she didn't seem to be getting any further along.

As Aub and I checked round the sheep we were kept abreast of the situation. As time went on, with our experience of lambing the sheep, we agreed it didn't look to be going too well and, fortunately, I was able to contact one of the large animal vets who would actually be passing close by our farm in the next half hour. By now it was becoming obvious that Aub ought to stay and assist Mark with what appeared to be his first difficult birth.

Farrowing should be exciting. Apparently, there's nothing quite like watching a gilt deliver a litter of little pink piglets, or spotted ones in this case. However, in a very small percent of cases, things don't go to plan. The majority of piglets are born facing forwards, but just occasionally one comes backwards or, as in Spot's case, gets wedged sideways in the birth canal.

I knew poor Toby was desperate to stay and watch the drama unfolding in the pig department, but Wilfred and Leo were raring to go to Crocodiles of the World so I bundled all three boys into the car and drove off towards Burford.

The whole place at Crocodiles of the World is amazing. We wandered round looking at Nile crocodiles and American alligators, giant tortoises and a Komodo Dragon, amazed at the size of some of the reptiles. While Wilf and Leo ran excitedly from one species to another, I was still aware of Toby's lack of participation, his mind being elsewhere. I really felt for him, but knew he was probably in the best place for a small child, if all was not going according to plan in the maternity department. After the tour we spent even more time and certainly more money in the café and gift shop, selecting mementoes of the day out, but that's quite usual. I decided each boy could have what he wanted, averting any dramas.

Pig World was not going so well. We arrived back at the farm to find Spot, not looking happy, but having given birth to three live piglets. Another three were dead in a feed bag. The fact she didn't have much milk was worrying, considering a litter of eight or ten would be normal. The vet explained that the trauma and antibiotics she was now on (hoping desperately to keep her alive) were having an impact on milk production. Fortunately, we had a supply of both baby milk and lamb milk powder. Unlike lambs, the piglets were quite happy to drink milk from a shallow tray and this, together with a heat lamp in a secured part of the stable, close to mum but safe, was to be the outcome of this farrowing.

Spot did survive and loved her babies, who seemed to thrive on a mixture of lamb's milk and soaked pig nuts. They lived happily together, with Dot in an adjacent stable, until it was decided that both Spot and Dot might like to return to their outdoor pen.

The babies stayed with us, in the stable. They were not to be named! But Bacon, Sausage and Chorizo ran amok around the yard each morning and evening while awaiting their next meal.

left to right: Wilfred, Leo and Toby at
Crocodiles of the World

Toby is our potential farmer

AUTUMN

John Keats' description of Autumn as 'a season of mists and mellow fruitfulness' describes our Cotswold hills and valleys so well. In the farming calendar, Autumn falls on the last days of August, and is both the start and end of our year. A time when we can spend a considerable amount of money investing towards next year's lamb crop with new ram purchases, and also sell our main harvest of shearling rams and excess breeding ewes.

I love the autumn sales because marketing is something I've always enjoyed, probably a throwback from my horse dealing days. I've always loved breeding or buying and selling. Selling from home is by far the most successful way of trading. Both Aub and I know what we value our breeding sheep at, and the negotiations can start from there. Buyers know their budget and we usually settle on a price and selection which leaves us all happy. That way, future sales are often assured.

In 2020, even though Covid was changing many things, most of the autumn sheep sales were still able to be held. These included the National Texel sales which Aub inspects at annually, although he elected to drive to Lanark with John and Ailish rather than fly there as they normally would, and declined the offer of inspecting in Northern Ireland.

All were held with social distancing and masks, and only the buyers were welcomed in the sales areas rather than the many spectators of previous years, but nothing was going to dampen the prices. At Lanark a new record was set by one of the top breeders for a six-month-old ram lamb, which sold for 350,000 gns, more than many pay for a house.

Moving on to the English National at Worcester, the only Texel sale I attended in 2020, he continued his exceptional run with top price, this time just 16,000 gns.

Aub set his heart on the best lamb in the Cambwell pen – even though, yet again, we didn't really need another ram. I had to agree he certainly looked the part, and although there were others we could have tried for, we decided to just bid for this lamb. Then comes the nerve wracking lead up to him coming into the sale ring.

When we originally sold at Worcester, the market

was right in the middle of the city, and getting there – especially for 'in lamb' sales near Christmas – was a total nightmare. The new market, in Nunnery Way lies parallel to the M5 with easy access from junction 7 and makes life an awful lot easier. Rows of metal pens line the concrete yards, most undercover these days. For the major sales, sheep are directed through the cattle pens to be sold in the main cattle ring. There are tiered stone and wooden benches surrounding this ring, where bidders can watch the proceedings and select their purchases.

With all the Covid precautions, the area was sparsely occupied, and by genuine buyers rather than spectators. Who else had their eye on this lamb? A number of people we soon discovered. Aub held his cool, not raising a bid until he was nearing two thousand guineas. We'd discussed how far we could go with the bidding but to our amazement purchased him before we overstretched ourselves. Another top-class ram to join the Haddo and Cornmore shearlings we bought as lambs the previous year. We only took two shearling rams to Worcester, but both sold well so all in all, a good result.

One thing that did improve with lockdown restrictions was the service at the restaurant next to the Premier Inn where we stay for Worcester sale. Seated at our table, our drinks order arrived far more quickly than it would have done if we'd had to wade through the usual hassle at the bar. We then placed our food order with our starter arriving promptly and our main course waiting while the dirty plates were cleared. Amazing efficiency!

When we first began farming all those years ago, there weren't many pedigree Texel flocks in the country. The breed was still new and selling the rams to commercial farmers, whose fathers and grandfathers had always used a Suffolk ram wasn't easy. As our flock grew, we travelled long distances to sell the rams, the Welsh farmers being far more interested than our local ones. This was mainly due to the way sheep subsidies were paid in the early eighties.

Hill farmers were awarded a higher payment, but the sheep had to be a hill breed. The Welsh sheep are tough, wiry little white-faced animals, excellent mothers and well suited to their habitat, but their purebred lambs are not the best meat types. Putting a Suffolk ram on the ewes, they produced a better quality lamb, but with a black face, which didn't qualify for the hill subsidy. A Texel produced an equally good, but white-faced lamb, and very few Defra men could tell the difference between a pure Welsh lamb and a Texel cross when they came to check and count, especially if they were halfway up a mountain.

Nearly forty years later – can it really be so long? – Texels hold their own without anybody needing to hide their pedigree. Sheep sales from the farm in 2020 really were mad. Very similar to puppy sales, although not quite to those extremes financially – we are talking about farmers after all …

Our Texel shearling rams sold well to commercial farmers as usual, but we also had numerous young farmers starting out, buying excellent females and good pedigree rams to go with them.

Even more enthusiastic were the buyers wishing to purchase Blue Texel ewes. Back in February, before we had any idea what was going to hit us, I'd had Mark T, our ever dependable assistant, who looks after our stock when we're away and helps out when needed, shear some of my best Blue Texel gimmers and young rams, with a view to showing at Three Counties Show in June. Sadly, we soon saw this was not going to happen as Lockdown was still in full force. But there were early sales to be had online, so I decided to select some of the Blues we'd sheared early. They would now be trimmed, ready to look their best online. Unfortunately, I didn't convey this message to Mark T when he sheared the rest of the gimmers. Those already sheared, after spending several weeks indoors while they had little protection against the weather conditions, were now running with the main group. Their coats were just reaching a point when they could be trimmed to enhance them, and Mark sheared them again.

After screaming and throwing my toys out of the pram when I realised what he'd done, I calmed down – luckily before I saw Mark T – simply having to accept we would miss these sales and it would be later in the year before I could advertise the ewes.

Even so, the first interested buyers appeared on the farm in May, so fed up with being confined in Wales and able to travel elsewhere for essential business, such as buying sheep. The ewes were all looking extremely smart, their recently sheared coats accentuating their lovely blue colouring, and their bodies so good that they didn't need trimming to improve them. I had never sold sheep so early in the year, but the phone kept ringing and it seemed foolish not to do so.

Aub and I went through the ewes and pulled off those we definitely didn't want to sell, mainly selected from breed lines where we might sell one of a pair of twins, retaining the other. Aub was not so decisive with the whites, mainly because given the choice he'd keep them all. It took several days of arguing for him to select sixteen ewes he had to keep, which when I counted them in the field a few days later appeared to have mutated into twenty-two! This still left quite a few really good quality ewes which we sold to new breeders, and we hoped would produce top class lambs for them.

Blue ewe sales continued, including some I'd previously decided weren't for sale. The trouble is, they are animals, and turning down a good price to find them dead on their back the following day is never good. Anyway, who knew what sales would be like in 2021. That good old farming saying 'make hay while the sun shines' is true in so many ways.

We sent rams and ewes to new homes from Cornwall

to Scotland, some sales more amusing than others. Our Scottish purchaser wanted photographs of a selection of rams to run past her ewes, although I think she made the final choice herself. He travelled to Carlisle with our good friends Giles and Sally, then continued on to Stranraer. Some buyers came to collect their sheep, still asking if we had any others to sell, and sometimes I found something. We supported the Society sale at Worcester, with two lovely gimmers finding new homes, and two ewe lambs going to families I knew would show them when we were able to get out again. This sounds like selling our best animals to our rivals, but we obviously cannot show all our stock so it was a delight to sell to others who will take them to major shows, publicising our flock. One family live close to the Royal Welsh showground, so I hope to see her competing there at some point.

The end of August and the beginning of September saw us backwards and forwards to Worcester market like yoyos. I think we could have set the pickup to drive itself. The English National Texel sale was on the last day of August and first of September, then we were back on 2nd with meat lambs, and 4th for the Blue Texel sale. Fortunately, we only had a few left to sell here, as we were totally fed up with sales by then.

Bluebell

THE PEOPLE ON
THE FARM

When our children were young, they were often involved with farming life, although this was sometimes more through necessity than enthusiasm. Especially when their father announced one Christmas morning that a large number of the ewes with a major eye problem needed to be injected with antibiotics, before presents were opened. I think I stepped in and said at least one present could be opened at breakfast, but could see why they lacked the enthusiasm their father has.

The latest generation of would-be farmers consists of Mark and Kate's three children, Toby now aged 11, Wilfred aged 9 and Bluebell who is only 3, along with our daughter Heather and Kevin's son Leo, aged 8. They all live locally to us and it's so interesting to see them growing up and developing good strong characters.

All three boys are totally different in their outlook on farming. Leo, once established at the farm, is happy mucking in with his cousins, often taking on a managerial role, telling them what needs doing, if he can remember from his last visit. He is fearless to the extent he needs reminding that animals, especially females with young, can be very protective and need to be given space. He has few worries about being in the thick of the action and loves bedding-up and feeding lambs, although rides in the gator and on the quad are still his favourite activities.

Toby, Mark and Kate's eldest, is definitely the most enthusiastic, capable of taking over the position of farm manager at any point. Prepared to help both his father with the pig enterprise and us with the sheep, filling endless water buckets and hayracks during lambing. He has an air of authority, needing little instruction to grasp the situation and can be relied upon in most situations.

Wilfred isn't such a great farming enthusiast. He doesn't really enjoy getting cold, wet or dirty. His great friend Ga, a limp, lanky brown monkey made of soft material, would usually accompany him when Wilf was younger. Ga was Wilfred's oracle, consulted at all times on all subjects. Ga could go home from the farm wet, dirty and smelly, especially if Wilfred annoyed his brother, which invariably happened, but washed and dried he would still go to bed with Wilf.

Bluebell is our latest addition and adores everything on the farms. She will run in with the piglets in the woods, trying hard to catch their warm, pink, squirmy bodies, then chasing after them, squealing just like a piglet herself. She bottles lambs and cuddling anything is a major priority, especially the dogs. No worries about mud or water, she just wants to be part of everything.

My husband Aub's favourite things are mechanical. That's why we keep sheep! He enjoys trawling through agricultural magazines, studying machinery for sale, noting when local auctions are to be held. The fact we don't need anything is totally irrelevant. He's a wizard with machinery. While we're usually better leaving Mark T rebuilding any stone walls, Aub is excellent at emergency repairs and does a great job on most other farm maintenance, although he does sometimes need psyching up to do it. Often better when he has someone helping with the job, other than me, although the right person isn't always available.

When fences need repairing, new stakes putting in etc. it's a different matter. We have to wait for Dave. A bit like waiting for Godot, although not quite as depressing. Dave is a friend and fellow farmer with a post hole banger on his tractor. Several other farmers we know have this piece of equipment on their tractor, often more available than Dave, but no, we have to wait for Dave. We've always used Dave!

Dave can have many reasons why he's unavailable; health problems, or sheep problems although he has so few animals now, I feel that's just an excuse. Could be weather problems.

'Can't come when it's this wet/dry/hot/cold' or a mixture of these. But we still wait for Dave, rather than ask anyone else.

Mind you, when Dave arrives every stake on the farm is re-secured, gateposts are knocked in and even holes bored through stone or concrete in the yard in the anticipation of posts going in. It has to be done at speed because it could be twelve months before we see Dave again. And there's no replacement for him. But that's life.

I'm probably just as annoying. I get a fixation about something that needs doing, and as Aub says, want it done yesterday. Well, at least today and not put off till tomorrow, or next week, or whenever Aub is planning to do it. I find it totally frustrating when I have to ask for something to be done at least six times before anything happens.

I also plan ahead. I prefer to map out our week, contact people we need in to help later in the week, giving them a few days' notice or choice of days to suit them, and start conversations about things that need doing later in the month/year etc. I now contain myself to discussing these ideas after we've fed and had coffee. This doesn't always mean this becomes a two-sided conversation, but stands more chance than if I burst out with my ideas when I have them. I have to store them in my brain, or write them down so I don't forget my plans.

I'm lucky if Aub knows what he's planning to do that afternoon, let alone in two weeks' time. Some years ago, when having an in-depth conversation with the bank manager about our farming plans, he asked Aub where he saw himself in five years' time. I waited with baited breath, and give him his due, he'd make a good politician the way he cleverly evaded actually answering the question.

Aub can to get depressed and grumpy if things aren't going well. I try hard to make him talk about the problem, which he's often blown out of all proportion, something farmers can do. Working on your own gives you time to think, and those thoughts aren't necessarily positive. Discussion can bring them back into perspective.

I'm the one who has sleepless nights over whether the dogs are cold in the kennels during a wintery spell, or holding the finances together. My saving grace is burying myself deep in a book, something that can also drive Aub mad. But we do work well together. Most of the time. Yes, we can argue, but mainly over minor things, like which sheep we will show or when we will move livestock. Anyway, if it's an important decision I can usually make it appear that it was Aub's, so it works.

Aub and Leo checking the ram
lambs in the 18 acre

SEPTEMBER

Some of our fields have interesting names – although some just boringly remind us of their size like the Nine acre and Eighteen acre. Others are really descriptive. Verandas is a large area which we split into several paddocks to benefit the sheep. Top Verandas is a wonderful vantage point for surveying most of the other fields, while Bottom Verandas is the lower part. Between them both are Middle Verandas and the furthest from the yard is The Ruin which houses stone relics of an old barn. Our final permanent grass field is called the Horses, and must I suppose have been used for grazing horses at one time, although no one can remember when. Maybe it was the winter turnout field for Pat's famous show jumpers.

On the top, adjacent to the measured fields lies the Quarry field – again, so named for obvious reasons

– and the paddock on the way to the farm is called Betty's field. Betty was a lovely lady who worked as housekeeper for Pat Smythe when I worked for her. Betty and her husband lived in the cottage opposite the field, and so the paddock was christened.

By September, the ewes have taken up residence in the 12 acre and 18 acre, so we have easy access to them for pre-tupping treatments. They will have grazed the Quarry field and Top Verandas earlier in the year, but both the big fields are secure so no stray ram lambs can interfere. There, the rams get on to the main business of the month – tupping.

September is a time of great excitement for the tups, or rams, whichever you like to call them. These boys live the life of Old Reilly with us, spending about ten months of the year lolling around relaxing, then a concentrated period of sex.

As the days get shorter and the nights draw in love is in the air, at least for the sheep and the breeding season begins. Tupping is a term used by the farming communities which basically means 'sheep mating'. Some farmers still turn their rams out afterwards, forgetting about them until the following season, leaving them to struggle on poor grass and maybe a bit of hay if they're lucky. Then they wonder why they are thin or lame when they need them the following year. Thankfully, these days, there are fewer farmers who treat their animals badly.

Quality stock isn't cheap and, if properly looked

after, a ram should work well for a good four years, often longer. That makes it quite viable to spend £1000 on a ram, if he's going to serve 50 – 100 ewes. The number he can cover depends on whether they are all set to lamb in one lot or, as we do, divide into February and April lambing.

We delivered two rams to a farmer who had bought from us the previous year, and he took great pride in showing us his previous purchase, which now looked like a bullock. He'd certainly valued his purchase and looked after him extremely well, and it made me very happy to see this. I couldn't believe it when another farmer contacted us from Devon because he'd purchased eleven rams three years ago and surely that was enough. But in fact, he rang to say all his rams were fine and he wouldn't need anything more this year, but had a friend who wanted to come to see our stock. Great to get a reputation for breeding good strong healthy stock – and he must be another good stockman, as it was quite an achievement to keep all eleven rams fit and healthy for four years.

On our farm, from the beginning of August the rams are given more concentrate feed, building them up for their busy time the following month. They go out with the ewes towards the end of September, for us to lamb in late February. A ewe's gestation period is five months less five days, for Texels we calculate 145 days.

For our February lambs, the ewes are synchronised to bring them in season at the same time, allowing us to manage a short but busy lambing session, aimed at around a week to ten days. We usually bring the selected females and ram into a stable or section of the sheep shed, to save the rams having to chase round the field.

The ram will have raddle (a coloured paste), plastered on his chest. He marks the fleece on the backside of whoever he covers so we can see who's had his attentions. It can be a hectic night for them, with eight to ten women eager for his ardour, then a break of a couple of days to recover before he's given a second lot. They all seem to have smiles on their faces when they're turned back out, the ladies to go in one direction and the gentlemen all back together to smoke a cigar and discuss things that men discuss.

Some years ago we put ewes with a ram in a paddock next to a three day event rider's yard. He trained some of the Japanese Olympic riders, and we were invited to their end of season party. They were interested to know why some of the sheep had red marks on them. We tried to explain, although aware their grasp of the English language was not always good. Suddenly one of them understood the situation, then rapidly explained to the others. After initial embarrassment, there was great hilarity when they realised the reason.

Sorting which ewes go with which rams can be stressful. We generally start with the whites and, as usual, this year, Aub has no plan. He can take a long time assessing each ewe, deciding which ram she'll go to, then wondering where to put her. I push the ewes from the back (the dividing gate can only send sheep in two directions), then as eight to ten arrive at his end of the race I suggest he selects which ram should go with that group of ewes. This rarely works to his satisfaction and we're more likely to fall out on selection day than at any other time of the year.

Time is usually of the essence, and as evening draws in, I point out I still have the Blues to sort. Eventually most of the ewes are in with the correct ram. I make sure to note all the ear tag numbers so I can be absolutely certain of each lamb's parentage. I dream of the day when we have an electronic reader, as neither of us has the best eyesight, and Aub is also quite capable of reading tags backwards, but they are expensive and we seem to cope.

In case anyone hasn't caught the first time, all the ewes will run out with a ram again two cycles later, after about 30 days. The commercial Lleyn X ewes will also go with rams then, aiming for end of March and April lambing.

We keep around ten to twelve rams, Blues and Whites, so we can offer purchasers different bloodlines. I don't like to think of one or two being deprived during the season, so we often put several rams in with the commercial ewes. We don't need to know the individual bloodlines for these lambs, like we do with the pedigrees.

Once tupping is over, all the older rams are put

back together in a small area, to dissuade them from swanking about the place, gloating about their triumphs and beating each other up. If the weather is really foul, as it was last year, they're kept in a bay of the sheep shed. As the weather improves, they move to a small sheltered field, where they continue to be fed and nurtured through the winter. It becomes a bit like a gentleman's club, lounging around, eating, drinking and sharing memories. Not a bad life. The newly purchased ram lambs usually join our homebred ones of the same age, again enjoying good food and a sheltered field, but avoiding arguments as might occur with the older rams.

The traditional annual Hop and Cheese fair at Worcester doesn't resemble its original title today, but is still a popular sale of breeding ewes and rams. The fair began in 1554, the original venue being Angel Street in the middle of the city, which would have been packed with hundreds of people as farming produce was sold, hops marketed and cheeses tasted. Imagine the sounds and smells of such an event. Children and dogs running around, while their parents marketed and purchased their goods. It thrived for more than 350 years before gradually declining after the first world war. The fair still continued in a small way, with over 8000 sheep recorded as being sold in 1952 – aside from the market records, we know this from the newspaper reports of lorries and livestock causing major traffic jams in the city. Now the market is based alongside the M5, it thankfully causes little or no disruption to traffic.

This September, we took a couple of Texels and Blue texels, selling them well, then ended up buying a Blue Texel ram lamb to run on for a shearling next year. A fair trade and great meeting up with friends and other farmers.

Due to Covid restrictions this year's National Sheep Association sale at Builth Wells was cancelled. This was a blow to many sheep farmers, as this is the biggest sheep sale in the country, with thousands of rams of different breeds being sold on the day. Consequently, the Texel society decided to hold two further sales, at Hereford and Llandovery. Aub would be inspecting at both, so we decided to take the last of our sale females and four rams to Llandovery.

The females sold very well, but the rams did not sell, just having an outing to Wales and returning home with us. They never seem to mind a road trip. I guess it relieves the boredom of sitting in the field.

A Blue Texel gimmer

EARLY OCTOBER

The last of the sales is Ram Friday at Ludlow. I always say we're producing too many rams if we have to take them to this sale, but in fairness, as long as they're good rams they make decent money and it's a sort of day out. Every type of ram you can imagine is there, from the smart Texel and Charolais to scrubby looking, unloved Welsh Mountain and some I find it hard to recognise. I quite like the mix of posh and rough, both in the sheep and buyers. As the auctioneer always says, 'there's something for everyone at prices to suit you all'.

We've been going to Ludlow for so long we know many of the buyers. It's always a pleasure when one tells us how well the ram he bought from us the previous year has performed well. There's nothing better than news like that. Some we know look at our sheep and announce they won't be able to afford them, even though I explain the cost-effectiveness of using a good ram, but I may as well save my breath.

Sometimes the weather is lovely, but more often than not the grey murkiness of autumn lurks round the pens. We arrive in good time for prospective buyers to view the rams, but time drags until the sale begins. Ludlow is one of the sales where a draw is made to decide the start. This can mean we're first in, before buyers are into the swing of parting with their money, or near the end, when most may have bought and gone home. Usually, however, we're placed somewhere in the middle. Once we've sold and passed on the traditional luck money to the buyers we hurry home, hopefully towing an empty trailer.

Luck money was originally given to ensure the animal sold went on to live a healthy life, and fulfil his breeding requirements, although nothing can guarantee that. Nowadays it is often just at the Welsh and border county sales that it is given, and quite often asked for by the purchaser. I always think if the shepherd has selected our sheep for his boss then he deserves a fiver.

Our oldest sheepdog Jilly was booked in for a hairdo. She was beginning to look very scruffy and I felt a groom and warm bath would do her the world of good. When I picked her up from Hilary later in the day she looked really pleased with herself, though slightly embarrassed. I thought she looked incredibly smart and her coat felt so much better – she must have been more comfortable. That afternoon on her slow walk up to the farm, she rolled in something particularly disgusting and looked even more pleased with herself.

Then more buyers arrived at the farm for crossbred ewe lambs. They came all the way from Derbyshire. We were under the impression they wanted twenty, but they took all thirty-six! Blue Texel x anything seems very popular these days.

Going through the ram lambs, we picked out four we didn't want to take on as shearlings and popped them into the final ram sale at Cirencester. I had rung earlier to check they were selling rams, but when we arrived there were no pens for MV accredited sheep. MV accreditation means that the flock has been routinely tested and certified free from Maedi Visna, a virus that can occur in sheep. Our rams would need to be held separately from sheep which were not from accredited flocks.

Jon, the auctioneer, rather inferred not to bother with the trouble of bringing our animals as 'there doesn't seem to be much interest' until he realised we had them on board. He then rushed round and bedded up pens for them and, after unloading, we went off for a coffee.

On our return we found several people looking at them, one farmer saying he needed a new ram as one of his had died the previous day. Tupping had only just started for the many April lambing flocks. I was glad others had registered that the sale was advertised as the final ram sale of the year. There didn't appear to be any other rams in the market, although later we did discover a couple of older ones on the far side of the yard. As Jon rang the bell to summon buyers to our pens, more people arrived and the bidding went far higher than we anticipated. We went home delighted. You can have very strange days at market.

While exports were not so busy this year, we did have an order from Henk, in the Netherlands, who had bought from us before, wishing to select two ram lambs for his breeding programme. Unfortunately, we only ended up sending him one, as several from our flock that conformed with all Henk's stringent requirements, appeared to be too closely bred to many of his females. His selection was a white triplet lamb, reared by a Blue Texel who lost her lamb, and was well grown with great conformation. One of the first crop by the ram lamb we'd purchased at Lanark, he'd inherited his father's looks and quality. Henk was worried about the chances of us exporting livestock to him after Brexit, especially if we had a 'No Deal', as obviously this was still an unknown factor in the government's plans, so travel arrangements needed to be in place before the end of 2020.

The month wasn't all rams and markets. My

publisher Lorna and I were sorting out publicity for my second book, 'Jumping Over Clouds' which was hopefully going to be launched in November. This required photographs for the press release.

I decided to try my impression of the lovely Yorkshire Shepherdess. I admire Amanda Owen greatly for her books, general diversification into TV, talks and self-publicity, aside from rearing nine children. She has really brought farming into the public eye, bringing home to people the reality and hardships as well as fun of family life on a hill farm.

However, I look nothing like Amanda. Whereas she is tall and elegant with legs up to her armpits, I am of a sturdier build, to put it politely. Another mistake was wearing my long navy 'funeral' coat, a gift from my friend Mary many years ago (previously a gift to her), and a better fit on me. It has come in very useful over the years and I imagined it would bring a sense of glamour, along with some bracelets and a necklace I found hibernating in a drawer.

There is a very good reason why I don't wear jewellery when farming: it can be dangerous. And I have the memory to prove it. Just before one of the English National sales at Worcester a few years ago, I've no idea how, but I caught my wedding ring on some part of a ram while trying to catch it, wrenching the middle joint of my ring finger. It was agony. Not that I was allowed to dwell on it, we had a further three sheep to clean for the following day.

With Aub doing all the inspections at the National Texel sales, it was always a bit frantic preparing our own sheep. I now insist they are cleaned and ready before he leaves for the first sale at Lanark. But at this point we were squeezing in cleaning between the Welsh on the Saturday and leaving for the English on Sunday night. Tempers were slightly frayed.

Gradually the pain started to ease and I continued scrubbing sheep, and packing up the car and trailer. Eventually we arrived at Worcester market, just as daylight was failing on Sunday evening. There was just sufficient light, some illumination left on, as the Scottish and Irish sheep usually arrive at the market on the Sunday night.

Having unloaded ours, given them feed, hay and water and made sure they were comfortable for the night, we headed off to the Premier Inn. Most sheep vendors stay here for this sale. By supper time my finger was aching, having swollen considerably and my wedding ring was feeling most uncomfortable.

Aub suggested I could pop down to A & E in the morning if necessary. He was probably right. Worcester Hospital is very close to the market; whereas our hospitals at home are at least forty minutes away from our rural corner of the Cotswolds. The following morning, with most of my left hand swollen and the finger looking like a salami, I decided I should be at A & E after I'd fed the sheep. They looked fairly clean and I'd have plenty of time to add finishing touches to their hairstyles on my return. Hopefully, by then, Aub would have finished the inspection and be able to help.

Unhitching the trailer, I drove the short distance to the hospital, checked I looked reasonably tidy, not too much straw in my hair, and walked into reception. The nurse looked in horror at my finger and immediately sent me through to triage. It was quickly decided that yes, the ring must come off before I lost the finger. I was sent to a cubicle with an icepack to try and reduce the swelling and await someone with cutters. Time passed. Trying not to sound impatient (knowing I wasn't a priority), I tentatively pulled back the curtain to alert someone I was still there.

"Sorry love," the big, lovely nurse looked most concerned, holding my hand and examining it again. "We can't find the cutters."

Worcester hospital is quite large. The staff were amazed that the mislaid set of cutters was the only pair in the building. I did offer to go out and see if Aub had left a pair of wire cutters in the truck, but this was declined.

"Your finger's so swollen, there's no room to use ordinary wire cutters."

The next solution, a hacksaw, had me worried. I was hoping to still retain the finger. Eventually, with four different nurses and porters trying to find the right piece of kit, a rather ancient pair of fairly heavy duty cutters, were placed in the nurse's hand. She warned me it might damage the ring.

It certainly didn't resemble the implement I'd once seen a jeweller use to cut a ring off a customer. Perhaps I was in the wrong place. The thought of driving into the centre of Worcester, finding a jeweller and somewhere to park seemed even more daunting.

My wedding ring wasn't particularly big or thick, but it did take several hacks to cut it and a fairly painful manoeuvre to open it up and remove it. My finger almost gave a sigh of relief when the pressure was released. The pain eased immediately and although the skin wasn't broken, I was offered a dressing to cover the finger plus a piece of bent gold metal that had been my wedding ring. Once home I put it somewhere so safe, I sadly haven't seen it since. How Amanda Owen works with a cascade of bracelets I don't know; they could make lambing a ewe a little difficult.

At my own photoshoot, leaning on my crook, or rather one of Aub's crooks, which was far too tall for me, I failed to look glamorous at all. More like Boadicea trying to flag down a chariot. I'm sure Lorna felt the same, although she'd be far too polite to say. Her photographs, as usual, were superb. It was just the model. My coat was certainly telling its age, bare patches were showing at the cuffs, and undone it made me look fatter than I actually am. My long scarf draped over my shoulders simply looked as if I would break my neck tripping over it if I did anything other than stand there, rather than adding a touch of class.

The final straw came when I showed my press release

photo to Aub: me, standing in a field, holding a copy of my new book, both dogs sitting beside me, with lovely autumnal scenery as background.

"Mmm, why are you wearing that silly old coat? Good of the dogs though."

"Perhaps we could cut off the top half and just show the dogs and my knees?"

Desperate, I made a frantic phone call to our cousin Ian, also an excellent photographer. He'd taken some brilliant shots of the sheep. My prayers were answered. The next day, once the morning fog had lifted, I wore a far more suitable set of clothing and decided to 'just be me'. And the dogs of course.

Typical of our life, I kept Ian waiting while I dealt with the final purchaser of rams for the year – of shearling rams anyway. Having now run out of shearlings we were delving into the ram lambs when late customers appeared. We must have got there by now.

The lovely Ian waited patiently and we drove to the yard, dogs on board. Maisie was first on the trusty quad, Jilly now needed a little help to climb up into the dog box. I drove out to the field to pose in front of the one remaining tree still displaying some beautiful autumn foliage. Every other tree had suddenly shed its most glorious leaves, leaving skeletal branches in their place; luckily this one was still hanging on.

Dressed in my tidiest wax jacket, I sat astride the quad-bike as normal with both dogs alert in the back.

Ian took some lovely, far more suitable pictures. Much as I would like to look as glamorous as Amanda, I have to be realistic.

LATE OCTOBER

Three generations of the Andrews family went to collect three Beef Shorthorn heifers, the start of Mark's beef enterprise. The grandsons wanted Grandpa to stop at the MacDonald's Drive Thru for breakfast on the way, which could be interesting with the trailer, but all the same I had no doubt Grandpa would oblige this time as he had every time before. Mark does not yet have his trailer license, although judging by reports in the farming press, I think this is now being abandoned, so Mark will be able to do his own collections fairly soon.

Aub and I had our own small herd of beef cattle many years ago. This was not intentional – I simply rescued five babies from a farm sale, where the purchasers wanted the cows but weren't interested in the calves. This did incur one problem with the authorities when I discovered one was unregistered without a cow passport, a document which shows details of the holding number it was bred on, its ear tag number and its parentage. The woman I was discussing this with on the phone assured me the calf did not exist. I assured her I was standing next to it, stroking it, so of course it existed. A protracted argument continued until I asked to be passed to someone in authority when it was all sorted out, but the memory stays with me.

As does the reasoning why we hadn't intended having cattle. Our fences were quite adequate for sheep but not so for cattle. They were destructive escape-artists. As it happened, someone had actually left a gate open when our calves, now ten or eleven months old, completely disappeared, but when we found them, their next trip was to Gloucester market.

Mark's farm was really taking shape, although it's purchase was very much a secondary plan. He had offices and storage for his computer business near Gloucester, but was become short of space for housing some older large servers. He'd been trying to purchase a larger building for several months. Each time he thought he had secured something suitable he was either gazumped or the seller changed his mind, which was irritating to say the least. When 100 acres of arable land with concrete pad housing four barns came on the market at a similar price to a building in Gloucester, his decision was made.

On completion, the land was growing wheat. It

actually produced an excellent harvest, something Aub thought quite impressive on the Cotswold hills. Not so Mark, who was horrified at the small amount of profit this gave him after a great deal of hard work and stress. A new project was needed. Now the arable fields are all in Countryside Stewardship, which pays far better than growing wheat, although does little to feed the country. Think of it as a kind of bee-bank. The fields are now full of wild flowers and clover, which look beautiful and benefit a variety of insects including bees, with several strips of land seeded to provide food for farmland birds, especially in autumn and winter and a large bare area available for lapwing nesting.

Mark's solution on the food production side was to keep a mixture of traditional breed animals. The woods were alive with young pigs, with a few older sheep grazing a couple of grassland fields and later today the cows would arrive. Sadly, they were not for breeding, as Mark had originally planned, but destined to produce the most beautiful beef to be sold locally.

Choosing the breed, making the decision to buy for meat not breeding, and general selection had been ongoing for many months. Many discussions about livestock took place around the kitchen table in both Mark's house and ours, the boys very forthcoming with their choices in the former. Originally miniature Herefords were top of the list, and these were definitely Toby's favourite choice, but proved difficult to find, some simply being small, full-sized Herefords.

Next in line were Dexters. A visit to a local breeder created a lot of interest. Aub, Mark and the boys were shown round a superb small herd of lovely animals, with excellent health status, definitely important for a breeding herd. However, after discussion with Paul, our butcher, Mark discovered the butchering costs were as expensive as for a larger, native breed, making it more cost effective to have something a little bigger.

Enter the Shorthorns. Friends of ours, Simon and Tina, run a Shorthorn herd, selling top quality breeding stock as well as butcher's animals and this also required a visit, plus lunch. As with our sheep, not all animals are of a quality to be sold as breeding stock but the meat from females in this category is delicious.

We'd recently bought several cuts of heifer beef from them and discovered the difference in quality between heifer and bullock meat – expensive, but melt in the mouth flavour and texture. Three lovely girls were selected, which had been beautifully reared and looked after for the first twelve months of their lives, now it was up to Mark to continue their wellbeing on his farm. The oldest would soon be ready to kill, but the younger two would stay longer, probably until we were so attached to them, we wouldn't want them to go.

The heifers travelled well and soon settled in their lovely field, sheltered by a belt of trees and full of luscious grass. Kate, Bluebell and I were there when the men and boys arrived at the farm, excited to see their new purchases. The ramp was lowered and slowly the first red cow looked around her; she seemed to indicate to the others that the place looked OK, and all three walked quietly down the ramp and wandered off to investigate their new surroundings. Later that evening Mark reported they were all grazing happily and seemed well settled.

Shorthorns vary in colour from white to red, with the lovely mottled roan much sought after in breeding stock. Mark's were a selection of red and roan – so attractive I didn't want to come to know them too well.

No names. Must not name those going for meat. Fortunately Spot's three piglets (Bacon, Sausage and Chorizo) were so well mixed in with some weaners he'd bought-in we wouldn't know who we were eating. The only other exceptions on the naming front were three bought-in gilts he'd decided keep for breeding – Bugatti, Porsche and Ferrari, known collectively as the Supercars – obviously named by the boys.

I know Mark is producing meat in the very best way possible, as we do with the lambs, ensuring a happy life with everything they could desire. I'm just glad we aim to produce as many as we can for onward sale as breeding stock, and the remainder are such a jumble, I can pretend I don't actually remember which are which when they go for meat.

A field of shearling rams

NOVEMBER

The month was grey and murky, when the fog rarely lifted, although occasional days started bright and sharp with a blue sky and a frost, from then on deteriorating.

Underfoot the texture of mud varied between soup and glue, depending on the rainfall, and neither was great when you're trying to feed sheep. Most mornings the troughs needed emptying before I could put the food in, a skill most suited to a game show. Sometimes overnight rain thrashing against the bedroom window had warned of this situation, on others it was just a heavy frost having now thawed a bit, still leaving more moisture in the troughs than the sheep needed, unless they wanted to drink their food.

The rams were now all out with the later lambing flocks. The main pedigree tups were back with the ewes who were meant to be early lambers, catching any not already in lamb and any other rams that hadn't worked so far this year out with the commercials. Hopefully the ewes would all take the tup rapidly and the later lambing wouldn't be too prolonged.

Adding to the gloom of the month, I lost my glasses. Not the cheap £1 ones I have for reading, but varifocals. I don't usually take them to the farm – in case I lose them! – but I'd wanted to read the tag numbers on the Blue cull ewes, just to keep my paperwork up to date. Deciding not to wear them when I walked up to the farm, as the morning mist meant I needed wipers to see where I was going, I put them in my jacket pocket. Sadly, I forgot I had a hole in the left-hand pocket. Well, if I'm honest I did remember – the pocket had disintegrated a bit and I thought I'd put them in the piece that didn't actually have contact with the hole. No such luck.

I had no idea when I'd lost them, only discovering they weren't there when I looked at my phone, which luckily was in the other pocket. I'd already fed the two fields adjacent to the yard, so after filling the bags of feed for North farm I returned to see if I'd dropped them in one of those fields. Oh, the excitement. Optimistic as always, the sheep thought I was bringing a second breakfast and I was mobbed as I walked down the trough area. No luck, although they could well have been trodden into the mud by now. When Aub returned to the yard I admitted what I'd done and he also went out to check, having assured me my eyesight without them wasn't good enough to find them. Neither was his on this occasion. He then drove me back up the Nine acre, the field I walk through with the dogs each morning. We could see where I'd walked as the frost was still glistening on the grass.

"Do you always meander around when you walk down the field?" he asked. "I mean, if you walked in a straight line, you'd get to the farm in half the time."

There wasn't an answer to that, and it did look strange following my route. I probably do this every morning.

Anyway, no glasses, so Aub offered to check in the home yard when we'd finished feeding. We continued the morning's entertainment at North Farm, then as it turned out, I didn't need to take him up on his offer – as my glasses fell out of the feed bag into the trough when Aub fed the ram lambs.

Just another morning. Just another day.

There are two important birthdays in November. The later one is Aub's and he doesn't like anyone to forget that. We normally have a family meal at a local restaurant of his choice, but with restrictions, not this year. He had to make do with me producing prawn cocktail, steak and chips and a banoffee pie that kept him going for a week. However, prior to that, Toby was eleven.

We knew he'd been saving up for a new bike and was

hoping for money towards this, but there seemed no shortage of others contributing, so Aub and I discussed whether it was time Tobes had his own sheep. Both our own children – Mark and Heather – had theirs at around that age, and he's so keen to help with the lambing, we felt the enthusiasm was there.

Mark asked him, casually, which he preferred, the Texels or the Blue Texels, and he chose a white one. Aub selected one of the April lambing shearling ewes which was running with the Cornmore ram we'd bought at Lanark, who had already given us a great crop of lambs. On his birthday she was dressed with a red rosette and TOBY written in red marker spray down her back. He's not likely to lose her!

We explained we'd keep her, free of charge, and he could either keep his lambs, if female, or sell at the sales. Once his one sheep turned into a flock, expenses would be drawn, but he could also move them to his father's farm. He nodded sagely, called her Mittens, and later she was scanned, carrying twins, much to his delight.

It's always so sad when one of the dogs begins to look her age, and Jilly was, although in honesty we don't quite know what age that is. She came to us when we were looking for a working dog some ten years ago. A shepherd locally, Rob, had been asked to rehome her as her owner had retired, passing his farm and sheep onto his daughter – she'd found that Jill wouldn't work for a woman and when she arrived she ignored me and

I ignored her. It seemed a good arrangement, but as I usually feed the dogs, she fairly soon accepted me as part of the farm and regime. And from there, as we often find with animals when food is in the offing, it wasn't long before she became a full part of the family, working as well for me as for Aub.

She's a fairly solid collie, with a thick black and white coat, the most expressive pricked ears and kindest of big brown eyes. Well trained, she's been a brilliant dog for us to have. Obedient to commands she also worked on automatic pilot when Aub stood at the gate and said "C'mon" which was his usual mode for sheepdog handling. His lack of instructions didn't faze her at all and they worked in harmony together.

She adored the quad bike, which was our usual form of transport round the farm before we invested in the gator. Once back at the yard she would still stay on board, so she didn't miss another trip. We often said that if anyone came to steal it, she might not guard it, but she'd definitely go with it!

She's always been wonderful with children too, something not all sheepdogs are, but she would put up with any amount of cuddling and soon sussed out that small children were a good food source. When Leo was about two, he rechristened her Lily Bicket, as she specialised in gently removing biscuits from his hand if he was foolish enough to wander round the yard eating one. Sometimes her first attempt at stealing failed, but not without perseverance, Jilly held onto it more firmly the second time and Leo would rush back to Heather or me explaining that 'Lily took biscuit'. She'd look a bit sheepish when scolded, but it didn't stop her, and she would never bite on anything other than the biscuit.

This year, when the November weather was inclement, she often refused to come out of her bed in the mornings, smiling at me and wagging her tail, but making it quite obvious that she was staying put! The dogs live in kennels with an attached run, their beds are a snug box raised on pallets. While Maisie would move back into the house at the drop of a hat, Jill loves her kennel, which is what she's always been used to. It is her sanctuary and she rarely comes into the house, unless to steal the cat's food.

Late afternoons, when I returned from feeding at the farm, she would be stood up and alert, wanting a walk before she had her tea. In the yard adjacent to our house many tons of wood have been left in stacks ready to eventually be chipped to feed the biofuel machine in the village, and the circuitous track around these log piles which we took most evenings reminded me of the old black and white wartime film, 'Twice Round the Daffodils'. At that time of day, once round the log pile was quite enough for me, if not for her, especially once we started lambing.

The odd ray of sunshine at the end of the month meant Jilly joined the morning walk on occasions, and she was always perky although took up residence in the gator on arrival at the farm. From there she still felt she held a supervisory position.

All this meant, though, that there was a vacancy in our working dog team ... just in time for Aub's birthday. We felt like we were joining the lockdown rush for a puppy but no – not a Cockerpoo or similar at an astronomic charge – a new collie as a birthday gift to Aub.

Some weeks before, friends and fellow Texel breeders in Dorset, Ian and Fiona said they'd bred a litter from their own two top class working dogs, and would we like one. Friends at Farringdon, Bec and Steve were already having one of them. As I was thanking them but saying no, Aub was saying yes, so he selected one. Black and white, with quizzical face, one blue and one brown eye, she'd been born at the end of September. After a long trip up from Dorset, with Steve and Bec's pup, she was a little quiet to begin with, having not enjoyed the travelling. She soon perked up, and we wished she was quiet again!

With Jilly showing her age it was a sensible decision, and she immediately bonded with Aub, who spoiled her rotten. We thought a good working name, Floss, would suit, but on meeting her, realised we needed something stronger for the type of dog she was likely to become. After much thought, and umpteen suggestions from the family, we hit on Jess and it suits her. It's just that I sometimes can't remember if I'm talking to Maisie or Jess as they are so similar in type.

Maisie is admittedly tri-coloured, with fawny

brown eyebrows and colour on her legs, but Jess is also short haired and similar in build. Her white legs reach halfway up her body, but as she has grown up her colour seems to fit her better. Typical of most pups, she was sweet and adorable, lived happily in a cage in the kitchen when we were out and at nights and was fairly easy to house train.

As she gathered her strength and enthusiasm the cat nearly packed his bags and left, although he then decided if he had to live with her, he'd better sort her out. Evenings were spent with this sleek black and white tornado tearing round the furniture like a wall of death bike, both pursuing then being chased by the cat. Jess would push her luck just so far, then have her ears boxed. She was quite capable of starting the day with a dust up with the cat while I was sorting breakfast out, and was even put back in her cage while we drank a cup of tea in peace.

Initially we had all the complications of her not being able to meet up with other dogs until she'd had her vaccinations, which it appeared she couldn't start for another two weeks. I then decided that the older dogs were vaccinated, and fairly soon after her first vaccine they were all walking together. Actually, walking isn't the right term. Dear old Jill was walking, trying to ignore the other two, who were racing around like lunatics.

Everyone settled in for the evening

Masie (left) and Jilly

DECEMBER

Both Blues and Texels have an in-lamb sale at Worcester early in December, so we decided we'd go and see what was there, for an outing really. It seemed a long time since we'd seen any of our friends, and with plenty of social distancing and wearing masks, we enjoyed the opportunity. After chatted to friends who were either selling or also on an outing, I looked at the sheep in the pens. Knowing none of the whites would be of interest, anyway we hadn't gone there to buy, I glanced at the Blue Texels, realising a breeder was selling up and had some lovely sheep in the pens. Finding a catalogue, I looked up the breeding of two I thought looked rather good, the older one having been bred by a friend in Devon. Pointing them out to Aub he agreed they were worth buying, so he slipped into the pens and handled them, checking their teeth and udders.

The Texels were sold first, then when the Blues came through the ring we sat on the front row around the smaller sale ring being used for the sale. Having discussed prices we went over our planned limit, but were still delighted with our purchases. Both were carrying twin lambs. Taking them home could have been something of a problem, but several friends had trailers with them, so they acquired a lift.

Another complication was paying for them. As we hadn't gone with any intention of buying, I hadn't taken my handbag or cheque book, and although we tried to pay with the farm credit card, the amount was over our self-imposed limit. Luckily, the staff knew us well enough to trust that we'd pay online when we got home – sometimes it's very useful being a familiar face.

Our other new addition, Jess was already showing us her intelligence, and constantly getting in the way, particularly when she was loose in the house. One morning while I was trying to go past her cage, which took up a third of the kitchen, she thought I was doing something interesting she ought to be part of and tripped me up. I fell against the plastic rubbish bin and broke the top. This, of course, instigated a search online for a new rubbish bin.

Note to all couples, never let your other half have a say in any choices like this. No, he didn't want another plastic bin, which I'd always found quite satisfactory and big enough to allow me to ask three times at least for Aub to empty it before it overflowed. Even then I usually did it myself. But no, he felt a metal bin, with top that opened if you moved in front of it, was far superior. We had to wait for one to come in stock, so coped with the old one without a lid for a while, but when it arrived I realised it was much smaller than the one I'd been used to. Aub, however, was very impressed with the fact it opened automatically.

So was Jess. It didn't take her long to realise that if she saw me put something in the bin, she might have time to grab it out again before the lid shut. Failing that, a wet nose on the front of the bin opened it again, allowing her time to investigate the contents before it shut. Great fun if you're a collie pup, a bit bored with domestic life.

With the puppy cage taking up so much room, the bin – which I'd christened Jaws – was sited near to the doorway to the downstairs bathroom, opposite the washing machine. Should I wish to utilise either, Jaws would open its mouth, making me jump until I got used to it. It was so much smaller than our last bin that I had endless struggles lifting the full plastic liner out without assistance, as it seemed determined to keep hold of it. Another strange phenomenon was hearing it opening and closing when in the sitting room and no one is in the kitchen. I've always said we have a poltergeist in this house; nothing harmful, just playful that enjoys hiding things in my office, that I then find in full view. Perhaps he's now playing in the kitchen with the bin.

As a younger puppy Jess also tried hard to give herself away. While puppies were being stolen, very kind people from the village kept putting her back in the garden when she jumped over the wall to greet them as they walked past. Hence the array of hurdles now barricading the garden, which we must remove before they grow into the vegetation and become permanent features.

With dear old Jilly simply overseeing the sheep management these days, Jess very rapidly showed her value as a working dog, really surpassing in the handling unit and pens, where Maisie is shy. Although still a novice, she can move the sheep through the pens to the footbath before I have shut the outer gate. She certainly has the makings of a top class working dog, and later we hope Dick Roper, our local sheepdog expert will take her for several weeks' training, when she'll hopefully learn to understand directional commands. At the moment I feel it is pure instinct which is great.

While we weren't actually under strict lockdown restrictions, no one was keen to go to Christmas markets, drinks parties or out for meals and I was finding it difficult to arouse any enthusiasm for the event. I'd managed to do the present shopping online, the weather was grey, and nothing was making the big day seem imminent. No school Christmas plays or pantomime trips. Everything seemed totally out of kilter.

On a visit to our local farm shop I did see a very nice, small Christmas tree in a pot and rashly bought it. This little tree could eventually be planted in the garden. I would happily just have put the green and red garland we hang over the fireplace and leave it at that, especially as it didn't look as though our grandchildren would be visiting us to admire a tree, but I knew Aub would be furious if I didn't get one. He loves Christmas as much as I dread it. I really do try hard to gain enthusiasm, gathering up all the Christmas cards to hang on the beams and sending plenty ourselves, but my favourite day is when I take them all down.

The little tree stood outside for several days before living on the small table in the hallway, where Aub sorted out the Christmas lights, which were a bit over the top for the size of the tree, and I added a few decorations. A few security items were placed strategically at the base of the table, around the power point, so a certain small black and white addition couldn't electrocute herself or eat the tree decorations, but surprisingly she didn't really seem interested.

Amazingly, we did manage to meet up with Mark, Kate and family a few days later – for their own Christmas tree hunt. We were able to wander through a small plantation of different sorts of Christmas trees for them to select the one they liked, which was then cut down for them. Of course, Toby and Wilfred had different ideas about which was the perfect tree, although both in agreement about the size. Large.

Luckily Kate had the casting vote and everyone seemed quite happy as they endeavoured to get it on top of the car to take it home.

I might have been struggling to find my enthusiasm for the festivities, but I knew I still needed to make sure all the presents were wrapped and food ordered. I refused to buy the size of turkey Aub always thinks we'll want but kept him happy by buying two smaller ones. One could always stay in the freezer until lambing, when it was ideal to have something to cut away at.

I was quite proud of the fact I'd found all the things the grandchildren wanted for Christmas, not difficult on Amazon I must admit, with a few extras I felt sure they'd enjoy. Children and spouses were also well catered for and Aub had a couple of surprises along with the usual socks, which he always seemed to like.

Sheep feed was in the barn, and we had plenty of milk and bread in the freezer, just in case the weather took a turn for the worst. Yes, most things seemed to have been catered for.

I knew the week prior to Christmas would be busy, but it did look fairly organised. I hadn't anticipated the dramas that were to unfold. The calendar on the kitchen wall indicated the ram going to Henk, in Holland on Tuesday 22nd was to be vetted at 9am Monday morning. The slight drawback was that I had a hospital appointment in Cirencester at 9.20. This was my chance to eventually see a consultant about the possibility of a knee replacement, something I'd been needing for several years. The appointment had already been changed from the previous July to December because of Covid worries with the hospitals. I'd cautiously rung to see if there was any chance of changing the timing, but discovered it would be postponed for a further two months if I did. Tamsin, our vet, couldn't change her timetable either so Aubrey would have to complete the paperwork I usually did. Looking back, I realise that if this had actually happened poor Tammy would have been filling in everything with Aub just adding his signature where he was told to!

Theo, our usual export contact, was unwell so he was sending another driver to collect the sheep. Other animals in the consignment were travelling from a collection yard in Scotland, then two picked up from Powys, with ours the final one to load. One other was going to Holland, several to France and others to Belgium on this trip with the route planned via Dover, sailing to Calais. Due to previous movements onto their farm the sheep from Powys, couldn't travel until midnight, so ours were not expected to be collected until 2.30 am now, rather than early evening. I always say export is not as great as it's set up to be, although on this occasion to be sending a ram lamb as breeding stock to Holland, where Texels originated, was quite a coup, even if we would be up late to wave him goodbye.

Apart from the change of driver and timings, all seemed to be in place until we watched the news Sunday evening. We'd been in the middle of enjoying a film, so it was quite by chance we turned over to BBC to catch the news, but it was lucky we did. Even by ten o'clock that night there were over 1000 lorries stranded at Dover, or on the roads leading into the port, and Monsieur Macron had closed access to France because of the new strain of Covid found in the UK. (At least, this was the publicised reasoning, although we, like many other farmers, felt he was firing a shot over Johnson's bows, warning what the situation of a 'No Deal' Brexit would look like. Perhaps we're just cynical.)

Whatever the reasoning, I was just thankful that our ram, and the others in the consignment, weren't stuck in that traffic jam. I realised the driver could have pulled out and turned round, but more travel hours would have caused chaos to his journey log, and what about the poor sheep? At 10.15pm I sent Tamsin a text cancelling the following morning's appointment and rang Aileen in Scotland who was directing travel proceedings. Already aware of the dramas, she agreed we should cancel the vetting, which only covers the animal for 24hrs and promised to keep in touch. I felt for Geert, Theo's driver, who obviously needed to get home to Holland himself.

Things didn't improve. We rescheduled everything and it promptly rained like a tropical storm. Flood warnings were out over much of the UK, and even on top of the Cotswolds we had roads running like rivers. Late on Monday the ferry from Harwich to Rotterdam was booked for the following day and vetting re-scheduled for Tuesday. Tamsin checked the ram was healthy, then we spent over an hour filling in the paperwork. At this point I realised that there would have been no way that Aub could have completed the necessary paperwork and had Tamsin had to do it all, the time taken would have doubled and our bill would have been astronomic. There are so many things that have to be completed for the export and much which needs signing and stamping, but in the end, to great relief all round, all went well. Miserden Debonair was collected and taken to Holland via Rotterdam, Geert the driver got back to his family in time for Christmas and the whole problem was solved more easily than we had anticipated.

Then, finally, came our own Christmas day. It was a strange time this year, as it was for so many. All suggestions of groups getting together for five days during a life-threatening pandemic seemed completely ridiculous. Then the news came that we'd be limited to just one day. As a family we'd already decided some time ago that we would lunch with Heather, Kev and Leo, while Mark, Kate, the boys and Bluebell would simply welcome Kate's father Rob, who would otherwise be on his own. We had considered all meeting up outside on Mark's farm round a firepit on Boxing Day, but as protocol sensibly changed, we cancelled that plan.

In all honesty, my immediate sympathy was with those in hospitality, like our lovely village pub. Having done a wonderful arrangement in the car park with marquees and fires to ensure everyone could comfortably have a meal while all social distancing, they were now faced with the news that they would be back to simply producing takeaways.

Life on the farm was so unaffected by the rules it was almost embarrassing. We simply got on with the jobs that needed doing, ordering farm essentials, collecting from the back of our local agricultural dealers rather than going in the shop, and making the occasional trip to market when essential, generally just to drop stock off.

That being so, even we didn't overlook the news that a new variant of the disease was causing concern and with the NHS facing their most dangerous of situations we were all told to stay at home. In the cities, it must have been so hard – that fundamental need for just one moment of fresh air – but I couldn't help the passing thought as I dragged on my wellies again, that given the choice I'd have loved to have stayed at home …

Then Christmas morning dawned bright and beautiful. This was a real plus for checking and feeding livestock, which obviously is done before anything else. We managed to exchange presents with Mark's family briefly, as all farming together we formed some sort of bubble, before visiting Heather's family. Having lunch cooked by Kevin is a delight at any time, but at Christmas he surpassed himself. I'm so pleased our daughter married someone who enjoys cooking. She isn't without culinary skills herself, but her enthusiasm for cooking is definitely lacking.

Being the family Scrooge I'm never the greatest fan of all the get togethers over Christmas, so quite enjoyed the fact we got the celebrations over in one day, especially as on Boxing Day the weather reverted to grey and foul once more. A comfortable chair in front of a log fire, watching the racing or a good film was heaven. For me the greatest excitement of the season is the shortest day, because I always think we can look towards spring. A bit optimistic I know.

A very inquisitive puppy

JANUARY

The weather as the old year ended and the new began could range from beautiful to horrendous in a matter of hours, let alone days. November and December had been so wet the only way to feed outside was with the gator and recently purchased trailer, carting most of a big bale of hay to the numerous fields full of sheep. At least the ewes hadn't had to come in yet. Lambing didn't start until the third week of February, so we were really hoping the main flock could stay out until the beginning of the month. I already had eleven thinner ones inside, on additional feed, and we had just started to feed nuts to the outside ewes, both the February lambing flock and the later ones. Grass was totally non-existent. I often wonder how we have these thinner sheep – all were gone through in August when anything looking suspect went, yet some still appear five months later.

Most mornings the grass was covered with a heavy layer of frost. This morning, it was snow frozen to ice. The dogs walked to the farm with me. You'd think they'd never seen snow, the way they threw themselves on the grass and rolled with their legs in the air. Once fully vaccinated, Jess was encouraged to ride in the gator, something she wasn't too sure of, with memories of her long trip from Dorset, but she soon became established sitting on Aub's knee, then happy to sit alongside him. Maisie was often in the back, considering this the place for proper sheepdogs to travel.

In the afternoons I gritted my teeth, walking head down against rain or sleet, round the adjacent field with Jess and the older dogs, but they seemed to enjoy it. Jill insisted on coming, when she could have stayed in her snug bed. It was an essential part of Jess's education, when she was learning more basic training like lying down and staying, and meant she was fairly tired during the evening, so gave the cat a little peace.

I do worry about the dogs living in outside kennels this weather, probably unnecessarily. Jill has a thick coat over an ample covering of fat (rather similar to me), and her bed is very snug and warm. Both dogs have enclosed bedroom departments set on pallets, their beds are lined with paper feed bags, topped with fleecy stuffed beds, checked daily to make sure they are dry and warm. Unfortunately, Maisie still hasn't learnt it was preferable to snuggle up in the bed rather than eat it! Her bed consists of a horse's thick saddle cloth, so far unchewed, with the remains of one of her warm dog beds. She seems quite happy, though I'm sure she'd rather be in the house! Jill definitely prefers to be in her kennel, and Jess is simply smug because she does live in the house, although she could soon be spending the odd afternoon in the kennel.

Saturday morning was cold but bright. Not the coldest we've had, but fairly chilly once the driver's door on the Gator exploded. Aub just touched the glass as he opened the door and it shattered everywhere. Not just the one disaster, he then managed to drive over some of the glass, ripping a chunk out of the front tyre. Oh, the delights of farm vehicles. It was Monday before we could arrange for replacements, so the old Ranger had to come into play. Luckily it obliged, the frost was hard enough for it to cope with the terrain.

I was amazed when the local John Deere rep told me two complete doors would cost less than replacement glass. There must be some sort of logic there, but it was lost on me. The tyre was fixed in a couple of days and hopefully the new doors would be with us by the end of that week.

Then we were faced with more winter logistics – gauging the cost of feed blocks versus feeding nuts. Which should we choose? Feed blocks make life easier as they only need replacing every few days and there is no major scrum as there is when feeding nuts daily, but after much consideration and juggling with figures, we decided the latter was the best option. We already had six tonnes of ewe nuts in the bulk feeder and this seemed the most beneficial way to go forward. As lambing approached the early ewes would be supplemented with blocks as well.

Every year, as the winter gets harder, it is always a juggling act balancing the right nutrition with the risk of overfeeding. While the majority of ewes, blues and whites, were carrying twins, we still had a substantial number of whites carrying singles, and didn't want them producing enormous lambs. The ewes carrying triplets and the one with quads would all be coming in when we vaccinated with Heptavac and mineral drenched, four weeks before lambing, when we would increase their ration.

Icy cold, the wheelbarrow wasn't balanced well with hay. More weight needed on left arm if I was to make it across the yard. Mind you, it was so slippery I was glad to use the barrow to either keep me upright or provide a softer landing than concrete.

Another national lockdown. Not unexpected. This country and the world have survived through so many of these disastrous infections: the plague, cholera, measles, the many different strains and variants of flu, smallpox, SARS and ebola, to mention a few. As farmers, we've seen Foot and Mouth and other animal diseases sweep their way across the farming community.

We've pushed on in the past, and we will do so again.

The last remaining meat ram lambs needed sorting this next week before they became too big to be of use to anyone. With lockdown upon us again I needed to check if Paul, our butcher, was happy to cut up and pack lambs for us, or if he'd decided to close his shop as he did back in March. At that point we used another local butcher, but the quality of presentation was so poor we wouldn't do that again. If Paul couldn't butcher and pack them, the lambs would have to go direct to market. It was vital that we retained our standards. We found that the trade for local, grass reared meat grew during lockdown. The anxiety people had about shopping in crowded places meant that they seemed to suddenly realise they could buy excellent food direct from farms and local shops, appreciating the quality and lack of food miles – and we've always taken our responsibilities very seriously.

Mark also had his first beef heifer ready for slaughter. Interesting to see how this panned out. Luckily, I'd had very little to do with his three heifers, so would happily eat his home-produced beef, but I knew Aub wasn't looking forward to taking her to the abattoir.

We both know all the arguments for kindly home-reared animals produced for this purpose, but it's a little different when you only keep a small number. I still remember having to park in a side street of Cheltenham to sob my heart out after delivering our first three lambs to the abattoir we used at the time. Mark's young pigs were also growing on rapidly, so I imagined pork would be on the menu fairly soon as well.

I found another ewe today in distress with sore eyes. We've been plagued by a pink eye problem. Clinically called infectious keratoconjunctivitis, this unpleasant infection causes considerable pain and confusion to affected animals, and can completely blind them if left untreated.

It is mainly associated with snow, but although we don't often get prolonged snowfall, on top of the Cotswolds, we can have harsh winter weather, and adverse winds and rain bring the same results.

A weepy eye may be the first sign, followed fairly rapidly by clouding, which can eventually turn to ulceration. Although we try to treat any animal showing symptoms with antibiotics as soon as we see the problem, it can be necessary to bring the whole field full in to treat. If possible we separate infected animals, so further treatment can be more easily administered, and hopefully those not infected will continue to stay clear. Once we're into trough feeding or even simply hay, contact can pass the infection on so easily.

Then suddenly, the weather was so much milder, what a relief. Misty rain, soft on my face was a pure delight. I caught myself really enjoying wandering around feeding, but remembered we must do something a little more constructive about sorting the remaining meat ram lambs. They were still in same field as last week, and it was time that the four rams running with the crossbred ewes came in. Lambing could go on forever if they didn't!

The new door arrived for the gator and needed fitting (not a one-man job), and hopefully the tyres were still up.

Where have all the Wellies gone? Does this remind you of a sixties song? Not quite so poignant, but still an important question. My left boot had been leaking since the beginning of January, but I couldn't find any new wellies anywhere.

Dressing to go to the farm became quite testing. Holding onto the radiator in the hall while I organised my left foot into a supermarket plastic carrier bag then into my slightly damp wellie, put a lot of pressure on my right knee, which was awaiting a replacement. Either my knee gave way or the carrier bag needed re-organising inside the boot. This often happened when I'd just checked the cameras in the lambing shed, seen a ewe with problems and needed to reach her quickly.

I popped into our local agricultural merchants, masked and social distancing, and was amazed to see so little on the Wellington boot shelf. Not to be put off, I felt sure I'd find something suitable, if not my first choice of boot. Not in size 7. In fact, unless I was looking for size 3 or 12, they had nothing. I asked when they would have more in, but the member of staff I asked looked vacant, saying she really didn't know. I hate to say it, but the staff of this establishment rarely seem to know anything. I did mention that the winter months are when farmers generally want to keep their feet dry, so perhaps there was a call for them.

But where have they all gone? Has Covid made everyone so keen to walk along wet and muddy paths that they're buying up all the wellies? Perhaps it's a bit like loo rolls and flour. Probably few have encountered a serious type of farmer's wellington boot before, strong, relatively heavy with a rugged sole. I imagine most would want the fashionable pink version emblazoned with Labradors or pheasants. I wouldn't mind these myself as long as they were the right size with some sort of grip on the sole, but most would see me sliding around our slippery farmyard, be it icy or simply covered in mud.

If the local agricultural store didn't have any, then surely I could buy some online. Amazon has everything. I got quite excited seeing the range to choose from, berating myself for not using this option before, until I again discovered all those shown were only available in sizes 3 and 12. Whatever has happened to sizes 4 to 11? I was even prepared to treat myself to something more expensive than usual. Aigle, I was told on social media, were the best. They were the most comfortable I was reliably informed. But not when the only option is a tiny size 3.

Perhaps they are all made in China? I presume this is where all the cheap dog beds come from. And therefore they're experiencing the same problems with shipping delays that are being reported in the news. After taking Jess to the vets for her vaccinations, I'd planned to buy two new beds for Jill, so they could be changed when one gets wet. The old ones I'd made tended to go lumpy on a hot wash, so these could be safely passed to Maisie – since, like the puppy, she thinks it far more fun to destroy a bed rather than sleep in it. No point in buying a new one for her.

Although, as it happened, she wasn't destined to have a hand-me-down either, as with none in stock it looked like poor old Jilly would still be utilising the lumpy ones.

One last search for the elusive boots. I spied some on Ebay. The expensive Aigle, but who cared about the expense now. Sadly, these are a private sale of size 6 which, with winter socks, I can't get my foot in, but certainly a better shout than 3 or 12.

No worries. It will soon be summer and the wellington boot shelves will be stacked again.

Overnight snow was quite exciting, making Sunday a tobogganing day. We must have had a good four inches. Mark and family borrowed the quad, and the entire family, plus small hairy dog and several toboggans spent an exhilarating morning on the banks. Then home for hot chocolate and a warm in front of the fire. Watching the morning news, the amazing lack of traffic on the M4 and M5 meant that the snow wasn't being mixed into slush with the grit left overnight, making travel even more difficult. Covid restrictions on travel may be working this morning!

Our dogs were in their element. Snow can be rolled in, shovelled along with a nose, then strange things under the snow can be jumped on. Repeat. Managed to turn our elderly pony Clemmie out this morning, walking through virgin snow gave a grip on the still icy yard. She was really fed up staying in yesterday after the yard became so lethal I didn't dare risk the journey to the field until today. I took some haylage out for her to eat as there wasn't much sign of grass, but typically she ignored it and simply continued to push the snow around with her nose until she uncovered a morsel of grass. We've had many cantankerous ponies in the past but she tops them.

The later-lambing ewes left in the Two Acre were demanding breakfast. I checked how many we'd left out there. Six. The hay rack was still full from yesterday, but that doesn't compensate for lack of breakfast nuts. The troughs haven't been used in that field for a while and were impossible to clear. Rain water that had turned to ice was under the snow, so I simply dropped piles of nuts on the snow. They found the majority of them and at least didn't spend the rest of the morning complaining I hadn't fed them.

Feeding was quite pleasant that morning. The sun even threatened to appear at one point, not with sufficient determination to penetrate the grey sky, though the early morning fog did lift eventually. Troughs frozen to the ground made life difficult. I watched with amusement as Aub kicked one of the plastic troughs, enabling him to empty the snow out, then taking a long time to replace it. I suddenly realised he was trying hard to restore the roof to rehome the mice who had been snuggled in the warmth under it. People often think farmers are hard men. Most have very soft middles!

The snow made life difficult with 42 ewes on Scrumps, a field some way from the farm, who needed to be on site for scanning on Wednesday. I hoped it would thaw next day.

The following morning I was relieved to look out of the window at green and brown. Snow is a bit like having guests – fine occasionally for short periods but definitely not when we're busy. It was suddenly incredibly mild, not that it had been excessively cold recently as we'd been spared the northerly wind, but our ever-present low cloud was still acting as a depressing grey blanket.

Scanning was planned for this evening and the ewes were still spread out around both farms. The February lambers were scanned back in December, with the majority having twins and only one set of triplets in the Texels although the Blue Texels got a bit carried away with five sets of triplets and one of quads. Still, this is better than seventeen sets of triplets and four sets of quads as we had a few years ago. The thought of endless bottles and pens with milk machines doesn't have the appeal these days that it possibly should.

The crossbreds were still on the Ruin, and Aub ran them up towards the farm instead of feeding them, as they needed an empty stomach for Rob to scan them accurately. There were also 40 ewes to come in from Scrumps, halfway between Sudgrove and Edgeworth, not the most convenient field for retrieving them. Now the snow had melted it was far too wet and muddy to drive in with the trailer to collect them from the small corral in the top corner. The only option, if we trailered them, was to load from the gateway, which we've done before with varying degrees of success. We'd try it, but I preferred to have a plan B should it all go pear-shaped.

Before he started feeding I suggested my plan to Aub who was impressed. As he agreed, he didn't really have a plan A, let alone B. He would move the earlier lambing ewes from the 18 acre into the adjacent 9 acre, so we could use the original field as a walk-through route for the other sheep, if necessary. The most direct route for home. Once he'd fed the ewe and ram lambs at North farm the fog was less dense and we decided that we'd scrap the trailer plan completely – walking the ewes quietly back to the 18 acre would be the easiest option.

Amazingly Plan B worked like clockwork. The fog lifted sufficiently, the ewes, in anticipation of breakfast were all standing by the gate and followed Aub with the gator and trailer. Jess was safe in the front, keeping a close eye on the feed bags and hay in the back. I followed behind in the car, hazard lights flashing, working Maisie out of the window. Whenever I told her to 'steady' she'd disappear, but I knew she'd be going backwards and forwards behind the car, bringing me on until I called her to walk on, when she'd chuff the sheep up a bit.

The road was clear, no traffic apart from one patient driver behind me. Often when we have to move sheep along our quiet country lane, picking our time carefully so that it falls after the local 'rush hour', the road suddenly inexplicably transforms into the M25. Most drivers accept there is little they can do but wait and often enjoy the highlights of country life, thank goodness, but the lack of traffic kept stress levels down, a definite plus that morning.

Once the ewes were safe in the 18 acre, Aub went back to the farm to sort something, while I tidied myself up for the dash to Tesco for our 'click and collect'. As usual the service was wonderful: all quickly loaded into the back of the car with a happy smile.

The sun was attempting to break through as I drove home, but our own personal cloud was visible as I approached Birdlip hill, incongruous, like a grey fur hat sitting above us. Back to dipped lights, I turned onto the homeward Stroud road, pleased that we now only needed to move the ewes back to the farm on our own track.

Rob and his scanning equipment came at half past

five, his long day still not finished when he left us. With Mark T's help things flowed well. Mark T could read the tag numbers, although he did complain about the lighting! I completed the paperwork and all went smoothly. Lasagne, made earlier, just needed heating up in the oven when we arrived home.

Scanning results meant the April flock should lamb at 160%, but this did include a total of 11 empties, the joint figure from February and April. Three of these will be given another chance next year as good young ewes, and when we synchronise, the drugs can sometimes mean the ewes don't come back in season, so they'll be given the benefit of the doubt.

Woo hoo, something to be said for old age, I had my Covid jab at one minute past three this afternoon. Nothing like being precise! The surgery was obviously working to a strict timetable. Mustn't be there more than five minutes before my appointment. This was in Stroud, not our doctor's surgery in Painswick, so I made an earlier recce. Didn't want to miss it.

We were forecast snow for yesterday but instead we had more endless rain. In the morning Aub mentioned that Eeyore, a Blue Texel ram lamb I'd bought in the autumn was breathing fast, first signs of pneumonia. He'd given him antibiotics, but with the bad forecast I wanted him brought in. This proved easier said than done, now the drugs had kicked in and he was feeling a little better. Having made the decision he shouldn't be out in either snow or rain, Mark and Toby came to assist in his capture. This still proved quite difficult, but did result in him being indoors for the night, boosted further with antibiotic and anti-inflammatory injections. I was glad to see he was fairly bright and chirpy the following morning; happy to eat his breakfast and stamp at the dog, so not feeling too bad.

Another casualty brought in out of the weather was a ewe lamb Aub had found cast the previous morning, having obviously been in that position for a while. He'd managed to help her stand up, but she'd been so wobbly she'd fallen over again immediately, so he'd tucked her legs under her and left her lying down, with hay in front of her and the circle of hay for the rest all around her. When he went back to check her later, she had moved, but was again lying down, while all the others were grazing, the downward position of her ears indicating all was not perfect, so she also came in for the night and was dosed. Next morning she was in her element, in with the thin earlies and those having triplets, enjoying breakfast and the hay ration. Far better to be safe than sorry though.

In the smaller section of the New Shed one of the blue ewes we'd bought in December, named Sarah after her breeder, was complaining loudly about her living conditions, the size of her breakfast or quality of hay. I leant over the gate and discussed this with her, pointing out she didn't need more concentrates, the hay was top quality and the barn quite adequate. I'm not sure if she agreed, but after a scratch under her chin and the conversation, she mooched off to try the hay again.

It was cold, a chill wind hitting as I'd walked down the fields, then again as I turned 'Fred Hunt's Corner' in the yard – so called as it always reminds us of the blast of icy air that hit us at the barns on Fred's farm in Througham, where we lambed in the seventies.

The result of these icy gusts meant half the yard was frozen like an ice rink that morning. We spent years dreaming of better facilities and now we're the proud tenants of a beautiful concrete yard, it can be a hazard at times. Thought to be level, we find that rain collects on the left hand side just a fraction more than on the right, which when frozen, fortunately means the right can offer a fairly ice free route from the stable to the field, if taken with care.

After feeding and haying everyone I discussed the weather conditions with Clemmie as I led her across the yard, pointing out that if she could walk like the decrepit old pony she is, rather than a Tennessee Walking horse, we might reach the field without breaking a leg. The situation wasn't improved by Maisie and Jess chasing each other in mock fights on the icy side of the yard, to strains of Bolero.

Clemmie, or Clementine to give her full name, came to us early last year. Heather had told me that some friends were borrowing her from Lynsey, an old school friend, whose children had outgrown her. I immediately mentioned that we'd be happy to take her on when the new borrowers had either outgrown or lost interest, but the speed with which she eventually arrived startled even me. A phone call was followed by her arrival half an hour later, with her entire wardrobe of saddle, bridle and rugs. The present family were moving away and the children weren't interested anymore. So, she now lives here, where she is ridden by our grandchildren and their friends when the weather is good and has a home for life.

We've had many horses and ponies, but I don't think we've ever had such a cantankerous pony as Clemmie. About 13 hands, a chestnut Welsh section B type, she is quite capable of refusing to be caught in the field by an adult but can give up gracefully to a small child. Not keen on affection from adults, she again appears to adore the attention of children. They can spend hours grooming and messing around with her; she's safe for them to ride, although ours tend to be on the lead rein still, and I gather she was a top class gymkhana and pony club pony in her past. When one of Toby and Wilfred's friends came to visit, who could ride fairly well, she was a safe conveyance off the leading rein, actually appearing to enjoy trotting and cantering around the field for a short while. But her walk is testing. She'd be brilliant to lead off a horse, but as I don't have one now, I feel as though she needs an Olympic athlete to keep up with the pace she'd like to set, hence the discussions about speed when I turned her out in the mornings.

As the foul winter weather set in, she still refused to be caught, even though I explained she had a dry, warm stable awaiting. She also managed to extricate herself from her headcollar on a daily basis unless it was put on so tight it rubbed her. Luckily, she came with two, and we had another ready, so when I managed to catch her, I could refit one, even if we were still searching the field for the previous one.

It does all still depend on catching her though. One day, Leo, aged six, told me he was impressed to see Clemmie and I were social distancing! Not from choice, I pointed out.

I'm not stupid with the pony – she's hardy and very hairy – but at her age, in her late twenties, I did feel she should be wearing her waterproof turnout rug even if she preferred to stay out at nights. However, with the relentless rain, she needed to come in at least overnight for all that thick fur to dry out enough to have it put on. She was also annoying Aub by standing near the gate, making the mud even deeper, ruining his field while waiting for her evening hay when we were feeding the sheep, still not allowing herself to be caught.

We hatched an idea. I persuaded her, over a couple of evenings, that the contents of my bucket were worth a look at, and even a nibble. At that point, again minus a head collar, she refused to be caught, but did grudgingly agree to follow me out of the field. Aub quietly slipped behind her to shut the gate and she decided to continue with the bucket, whose contents looked quite appetising, and followed me into the stable. Two days later she'd dried sufficiently so I was able to fit the waterproof rug. She returned to the field in an ill-fitting old headcollar, hanging too low over her nose, but which she's never tried to remove. Her coat was really matted, but no permanent rain scald damage.

As winter progressed and the field struck me as an unpleasant place to spend a night, I gradually persuaded Clemmie to come in for a small handful of nuts instead of just the hay thrown over the wall. Not totally convinced and still unwilling to be caught, she did condescend to follow the bucket, then let me catch hold of her headcollar before we met the concrete. With this regime she stayed well away from the gateway until I called her, improving that muddy area somewhat, so it was win-win all round.

Clemmie on a cold morning

FEBRUARY

The phone wasn't working. Being cordless, to actually find it was a plus, as when it rings we can spend so much time trying to locate it our caller has given up. This time, although I had it secure in my hand, the screen was black. I attempted to revive it with a good slam on the home hub thing, but life was extinct.

Next came the raid through the kitchen drawer of all the useful things we'll need some time, half of which I can't even name. Eventually I found a new pack of triple A batteries, which took several attempts with a sharp implement to remove from their impossible wrapping. I inserted them with the usual difficulty. Bright and alert the phone sprung back to life, but was searching for its hub, so I replaced it. After lunch I mentioned what I'd done and suggested Aub sifted through the 'really useful things' draw and got rid of what doesn't comply.

"So, they said non-rechargeable, did they?" he asked.

"Yep."

"And what have you done with the phone now?"

"It's in the hall, on the hub."

"You mean the charger?"

"Weeell, yes I s'pose so. Oh. Do they need to be re-chargeable ones?"

Aub said yes, they probably did. No, the village shop was unlikely to have any and yes, perhaps I should remove the phone from the charger before I blew the house up. I think he was exaggerating! It actually carried on working for another twelve hours. I ordered some rechargeable batteries online (since we were, as ever, still in lockdown), hoping they'd be here the next day. Life can get confusing, can't it? And no, he had no intention of looking through the 'really useful things' draw, because he wouldn't expect me to recognise any of the vital items.

I was obviously late this morning. Aub was driving towards me up the adjacent 18 acre field to feed the ewes, before I'd even hit the footpath on the 9 acre. When he leaves in the morning, I often take the opportunity to read a bit more of my current book; I must have read for longer that day.

I could see the ewes following the gator and trailer in an orderly fashion, single file as he drove up the field. He got out, picked up their bag of nuts from the trailer and walked on dropping feed in piles as he went. There was no scrum or rush, they simply followed him like the good-mannered animals I know they're not. I must have a different technique as I'm usually flattened by the time I've dropped the first three piles. Driving halfway up the field is probably the clue to his success.

Then Aub couldn't find a route across bottom Verandas to the Ruin without going through a bog. It didn't help that it must have rained again last night. He was feeling a bit down anyway. Maybe something to do with me suggesting he cleared out the Bike Shed. When we first moved to the farm, we lambed eighty sheep in there, now I'd struggle to stuff three in the doorway. There are also lots of things he can't find. We both expect me not to be able to find things, but when Aub can't, it's a bit more serious. With Ben's help he started clearing it and was amazed by what had already surfaced.

I went in there this morning to fill the water containers in the New Shed with the hosepipe and found the tap immediately, instead of fighting through feed bags and tripping over the airline. Wonderful. Both Ben and Mark T were set to help him continue the work so I anticipated all sorts happening.

Then the next day – tragedy. My beautiful Cornmore ram died. Barely two years old. We'd had the rams in since they came away from the ewes; the fields were so wet it seemed pointless leaving them out in the mud and rain. In the shed, Cornmore appeared to have taken a chill which was successfully treated with antibiotics and steroids. With a slight improvement in the weather, we thought it best to turn them out, obviously not. I cannot believe that my beautiful Lanark purchase is no more.

He was a bit of a thug, never afraid to thump me when I fed the rams, but he was terrific. An eye-catching head, with beautiful dark tear ducts, which I appreciate on prime lambs is of no use to anyone, but on pedigree Texels, especially females, is a major selling point. Not very tall, but with length, lovely top line and superb, muscular back end. He left us sixteen lambs last year and thank goodness we're expecting thirty-six this year. All natural service, which proved his prolificacy. Two of last year's ram lambs were sold; one for the Texel Society's breeding trials and the other, Miserden Debonair, to the Netherlands. I can look forward to this year's lambs, but feel totally gutted at losing him.

He was such a character. When he came home from Lanark, he showed his disapproval of our ram feed mix, demanding something considerably better, and more of it. Had I'd complied he'd have eaten a good six pounds of food a day and still looked for more!

Some years ago we had a similar disaster with a 'Cowal' bred Texel ram lamb we bought, Sundancer. Of similar type with a wonderful head, dark tear ducts and tremendous body, he'd died at around the same age. In this case it was a double tragedy; we found my Little Whiskers Blue Texel ram, the same age, dead the following day. All our rams and ewes are vaccinated for Pasteurella annually, the younger ones twice a year. Cornmore had his most recent vaccine two weeks ago. Sadly, Pasteurella takes more forms than there are vaccinations. Like most sheep, it's difficult to know all the reasons. He was my pride and joy among the white Texels. I was heartbroken.

We sent Cornmore to Guda, our investigatory vet, to take a brain sample, needed to conform to the scrapie monitored scheme, enabling us to export, but also for a post mortem. Knowing for certain whether it was pneumonia or laryngeal chondritis, which affects the upper respiratory tract, or something else, and whether we could have treated him differently, can only be helpful for future situations.

The results arrived at the end of yet another grey and miserable day. Farming is always about the ups and downs but why is it that grim news always gets mirrored by the weather? You can understand why farmers, especially those living solitary lives, can suffer from depression.

Guda's post mortem indicated it may have been a fight with another ram that killed Cornmore, not Pasteurella at all. Either way it was a sad loss. I hoped he'd produce a good son to take up the mantle. Thank goodness it was Friday and I could open a bottle of wine.

Then, unexpectedly, we had sunshine on Saturday. I feel that this is always something to be noted in January and February. It always raises my spirits. Jill wasn't impressed though. She decided it was a duvet day again and was not leaving her snug bed in her kennel. After yesterday's afternoon walk she opted to go back to the farm later with Aub and Maisie, so probably overdid it. There's no logic to the way her brain works these days. She was perfectly happy to join today's afternoon walk round the nine acre, even showing aggression to some poor innocent dog out with his owners on the footpath.

Even with sunshine the cold east wind was strong enough to whip the gate from my hands as I went down the 9 acre. Maisie is great with Jess, letting her play and join in with everything in the yard, but as we walk down to the farm she regularly duffs her up, asserting her superiority.

The wind eased, then suddenly caught me with such force it almost lifted me off my feet. Thank goodness it was coming in this direction, a west wind this cold would freeze the water troughs in the main sheep shed.

A few weeks ago I suggested it would be good to get the rubbish balanced on some walk-through feeders in the grain store cleared out. I'd mentioned this several times over the past few years, to no avail. This time I encouraged Ben, who's been helping us, to asked Aub if he'd like a hand to do it, and it actually happened. A trailer load of fencing rails went to Mark's farm, scrap went in the skip and anything useful, and apparently several useful items were found, were re-housed. We reclaimed about 150 square feet in the grain store and the walk-through feeders were established in the New Shed, making feeding in there a doddle.

No rugby scrum to deal with anymore. Just the hazard of tripping over old Mrs Lleyn's long neck and nose when trying to distribute hay. She's convinced if she searches right to the far side of the feeder there'll be a stray sheep nut all the others have missed and who am I to disillusion her? The haylage was tough that morning, really didn't want to come apart to shake out into the feeder and racks. Another good reason why my nails are so short, though they still manage to rip. How some of my friends with the same feeding routine keep their nails so perfect I don't know.

I have my friend Mary to thank for the fact that for once I got to listen to a radio programme I really wanted to hear – a repeat of Jilly Cooper's Desert Island Discs, which I listened to over coffee. Mary sent me a text, I'm hopeless about knowing what's on the radio and often miss some really good things.

Some years ago, I remember Mary and I went to 'meet Jilly Cooper' at the Cheltenham Lit Festival. which was most entertaining. Jilly advised writers to keep a diary, as you never remember what happened yesterday, which is so true. Also to use the senses, which I always try to do, so I must be doing something right.

Inspired by her radio playlist, I sat down and

wrote the synopsis for a new novel, one of Jilly's music choices having sparked a memory. Then I reverted to my student days, dusting off a leftover pizza from the fridge and heating it in the microwave. I think I was better at timing as a student – this time it flopped onto my plate in a very unappetising manner, but I still ate it.

I've been trying quite hard to sort out diets and good healthy meals – farming life always seems to make mealtimes a rushed afterthought – but with internet searches turning up recipes like Harrisa-spiced prawns with baba ganoush & quinoa, spicy Mexican turkey, coconut rice and lime and Massaman beef steak curry with roasted butternut, I'm wasting my time. They all sound delicious to me, but no chance for my 'set in his ways farmer' who simply likes meat and two veg.

So, as if to prove the point, that night we had a roast half-leg of delicious Miserden Texel free range lamb. No, we don't usually eat the profits (this would sell at the Green Shop), but a lovely lady from neighbouring Bisley asked me for a photograph of a roasted joint to illustrate an article she's writing for the local magazine, about a No Air Miles Easter lunch, which would include our lamb. Finding myself without a picture and purely for publicity, we were forced to enjoy the leg of lamb that evening. Luckily, I did remember to photograph it first.

MID FEBRUARY

Looking at February in my diary, the majority of my notes seem to be about the weather: I'm getting as bad as Aubrey, whose main topic of conversation is often the weather forecast. 'Cold, although other parts of the country seem worse off than us ... Had a slight sprinkling of snow, which only resembled a hard frost ... The wind was sharp, but far more pleasant outside than I'd thought it would be ...'

The trouble is the weather makes so much difference when you work outside, not only a physical difference but mentally. Once the grey fogs of winter descend on our hill it can be hard to gain the enthusiasm a sunny day will bring. Then suddenly the sky will clear and everything improves.

I was wandering around the yard feeding those that were in, just congratulating myself for everything going well as I fed the later girls in the sheep shed, when I walked back past the New Shed to discover that my Blue ewe, who was due to have quads, had a waterbag hanging out.

Why do they do this? It was over two weeks until she was due to lamb. As she wasn't doing anything that looked vaguely like participating in producing children, I dash to the vets for a drug that hopefully helps to dilate the cervix, aimed at making things easier later. The chances of success and live lambs is virtually zero, but saving the ewe is paramount.

Both older sheepdogs are due for vaccination boosters, but when I enquire if it's possible to bring them down with me the small animal receptionist is horrified that I should think that viable. The vaccination clinics are well booked up until the second week in March. Should we have to have a vet out during lambing she'll see if they can bring the dogs' vaccine with them, but it's unlikely. Neither dog appreciates the 20 mile round trip to the vets.

Even after administration of drug to dilate the cervix, not a lot of enthusiasm from the little Blue ewe, so Aub investigated. At least now he could get a hand inside, with me holding her with my feet. If I get down on my knees I might never get up again. He eventually managed to extricate three perfectly formed ewe lambs, with heart beats, but never taking a breath. It's so sad. They were just so premature their lungs weren't sufficiently formed to allow them to breath. All incredibly difficult to get out, tangled with the placenta, and after attempting to find a fourth unsuccessfully, Aub decided not to investigate further. All scans aren't accurate, especially with multiples. After a large dose of antibiotics, she settled down to recover, but the following morning looks ominously like she's trying to push her uterus out. Luckily vet, Louise, managed to get to us incredibly quickly.

I was all organised for once. Checked the hot water tank was on in the milk shed and the cold water running as well, neither of which had worked the day before. When Louise arrived, I rushed off to fill a bucket with warm water and find some clean towels. Well, the hot water tank had lied. It was on, but only gave us about a teacup of warm water. Likewise, the cold tap looked enthusiastic for a few minutes, allowing me to part fill and boil the kettle, then refused to offer any more water to make the contents of the bucket the right temperature. Not to be thwarted, I found a metal mallet head and cracked the ice on a bucket of clean water in the yard as a solution.

Louise investigated the problem with her usual care and attention. Replacing the uterus was not straightforward and she was concerned it had ripped, but eventually realised one uterine horn had folded inside the other. I ran, or rather shuffled awkwardly with my bad knee, to the shed for slip jel. Water was pouring into the sink, I turned off the thawed taps and returned. Deep down in the inside horn Louise found the fourth lamb. She could quite understand why Aub couldn't feel it, and took a while to get it out, having replaced the uterus. My poor ewe. What an experience for her first pregnancy.

Dosed to the eyeballs with anti-inflammatories and painkillers and given a twin lamb drench as she hadn't eaten that day, we left the little ewe to quietly recuperate. She would need more antibiotics for the following four days, but hopefully would fully recover.

Not to be. Everything had been too much and just after lunch Aub found her dead. Sheep are such stoic fighters, the Texel breed especially. They often amaze us with their ability to rebound from a near disaster. Sadly, not today. There are days when I hate farming.

I really think in a former life I was a creature who hibernated for the winter months. I've probably got enough fat reserves to do this now, appearing in May with a slimmer figure.

So cold. Bitterly cold. On Wednesday 10th we all spent the greater part of the day thawing out water. Luckily the troughs at North Farm weren't frozen solid, those fields being that bit lower and warmer than at Sudgrove. At Sudgrove and Mark's Bisley Lane Farm everything was frozen. Mark and Toby appeared in our yard around nine o'clock, the water they'd taken from home having been drunk by the cows and the pigs had buried their water troughs in now frozen straw. We'd have to wait until Aub came back from feeding the ewes;

he'd manage to thaw out a tap to fill the containers.

Not much help on the thawing front, I was more like the sorcerer's apprentice, carrying endless buckets of water to animals too far away from the short piece of thawed-out hose. Aub and Mark were out until 8pm still attempting to get water running to the pigs at Bisley Lane and the sheep at Sudgrove.

The next day, the night's battle against the frozen pipes made things a little easier. Occasionally the wind dropped and the weak winter sun came out, but the wind simply changed direction rather than disappearing.

Someone sent me a copy of *The Good Wife's Guide* on how to treat your husband, from Housekeeping Monthly, 1955. It's wonderful. I'm sure we should all treat our farming Other Halves like this. *'Having his dinner ready when he gets in is the best way to let him know you've been thinking about him and are concerned for his needs'.* (Impossible, we usually come in at the same time.) Even better, the wife takes fifteen minutes to rest, so she'll be refreshed when he arrives home. *'Ideally she will have touched up her makeup and put a ribbon in her hair.'* (Oh yes.) *'Be gay and interesting for him. His boring day may need a lift and one of your duties is to provide it.'* Ok, I'll try. As we've probably been working together all day this could prove difficult!

'Clear away the clutter, making one last trip through the main part of the house with a duster before he arrives.' (Clear away all the Farmer's Weeklys and other papers

from his side of the table and he'll be moaning and searching for something vital.)

'Light a fire for him to unwind by.' Well, I'm all for that, providing he's chopped some kindling, before I'm expected to feed it with tree trunks. *'Greet him with a warm smile and show sincerity in your desire to please him. Speak in a low and soothing voice.'* Wow. *'Arrange the cushions and offer to take off his shoes.'* Yuk, no thanks.

And the best bit, on which Aub often feels I let him down, *'Don't ask him questions about his actions, or question his judgement or integrity. Remember, he is the master of the house, and as such will exercise his fairness and truthfulness. You have no right to question him. A good wife always knows her place.'*

"I never question your judgment or integrity," I said.

"No. But you usually make a decision then somehow twist it round to look like it was mine!"

We agreed it generally worked okay, and no I'm not going to arrange his cushions or take off his wellies.

However, bearing the former instructions in mind I decided to be a domestic goddess that afternoon, making pastry for a pie for supper and vacuuming the carpet, where the delightful Jess had strewn the remains of her teddy's stuffing and numerous half-chewed sticks she'd bought in. I hate housework, but when the machines rebel it's even worse. The Dyson refused point blank to consume any more teddy stuffing. I could feel for it, we've had this toy's innards strewn all over the floor for weeks, however, once I'd picked up the bigger bits, the Dyson still wouldn't co-operate. It pretended to suck up the smaller bits then sick them out a few inches further along the carpet, and stick was a definite no-no. I'd be better off with the yard brush. Eventually the carpet looked a little better and I knew pie for supper would score. I'm obviously getting the hang of this Good Wife thing.

Valentine's Day. I didn't even hear the alarm this morning, or notice Aub getting up, but came down to discover a special breakfast. Poached eggs on toast. Yummy. This is his speciality and I'm useless at making them, probably what spurred him on to cultivate the skill.

I was late to bed last night waiting for our elderly cat to come in. Why he had to be so stupid as go out for a wee when Jess went out for a last run, I have no idea. Obviously, he couldn't come back in with the puppy, but he's too old to leave out on a freezing cold night. Aub was already asleep after another tough day.

Dragging on my wellies still involved balancing on one leg, sadly the one with the gammy knee, trying to adjust my Tesco's carrier bag in my left boot. Please could someone get new wellies back in stock? Any price considered.

I suppose everything outside was beginning to thaw a bit, but still just as unpleasant. Horizontal icy shards of rain hit my face as I walked to the farm. Jilly opted for another duvet day; I really couldn't blame her. Checked she's fine and snug in her bed, and left her with some breakfast, which she'd eaten by the time we returned from Sudgrove.

Then suddenly it was ten degrees milder. Sadly, typical pneumonia weather for sheep. It takes them a while for them to adjust to these changes of temperature. The birds were delighted though, it had been weeks since I'd heard the symphony of calls around the yard. Loud and piecing, short and repetitive trills. They'd had a rough couple of weeks with this cold weather, although plenty of access to grain in our yard. Aub even bought meal worms for them. They were obviously very happy as they were still singing late in the afternoon when we rushed to get the ewes in. The first of the ewes were due to start lambing in about seven days' time. We couldn't get them in any earlier today as they were still wet from yesterday's frost and ice, but the morning sun has done its job.

After much discussion about the age and cost of repairs to the old gator, we had decided to trade her in for a new model and Aub was picking that up this afternoon, so it was almost dark by the time all the pregnant ladies were in the barn.

During the evening I realised it was time to change my socks. Now it had warmed up, the Norwegian ones, a lifesaver over the last couple of weeks, definitely needed replacing for thinner socks, before I melted. (I do have several pairs, I hasten to add. I just mean I'd been wearing the same type of sock for some weeks …)

And then, just for a change, the rain came back. Lashed against the bedroom window last night, waking me up. Not so Aub, absolutely knackered after another long day. Thank goodness we got the ewes in while they were dry. A busy day ahead with Mark T drenching shearlings who were looking a bit dirty. Then they sorted the ewes into singles and doubles and put up lambing pens in the grain store.

I was getting quite worried as this was Jilly's third duvet day. Last night she was quite odd, barking in the evening. When Aub went out to check her, she wanted to come into the house. I found some special biscuits, but she didn't want to stay inside, so returned to her kennel. She's warm and snug there. Again, Jilly started barking in the night, around midnight. I leant out of the window and shouted to her and she went quiet. I don't know if senility makes her wonder where she is. There are lights on in the yard, so she can't feel trapped in the dark.

Hopefully she went to bed and slept from then on. She was as bright as a button by breakfast-time. When I arrived at the yard I was really impressed to find Aub and Mark T had got all the lambing pens up in the grain store. Incredible. Most years I've stood waiting with a ewe and two lambs while the first pen was built.

Moving sheep can be a total fiasco sometimes – this was one of those moments. A friend's daughter, Ellen, wishes to go to vet college and wanted to experience lambing, so came to visit our setup. Too early for anything to be happening, although in other years we could already have had three or four lamb by now. It's at this point every year I panic that I've got my dates wrong. So far I never have, but quite unusual for no one to decide to lamb early, other than my poor blue ten days ago. At least anything doing it now should quite happily survive.

Taking Ellen on a guided tour of the sheep shed and newly laid-out pens, I suggested she might like to sweep up the excess straw in the walkways between the rows of pens while I turned Clemmie out. That was when I realised the later lambing ewes had managed to open their gate and were heading off to the fields. The sun was shining and they obviously thought they'd been inside too long. There was little I could do. Aub would have left all the gates open to the bottom fields, as there were no sheep out there, so I simply shut the yard gate as the last large white fluffy backside skipped off into the distance. With a dog we'd get them in later.

As there was so little I could show Ellen – the 'milk' shed not being tidy enough for me to lay out books etc and lambing kits – I decided she could help me sort the remaining ewes into singles and doubles to aid the feeding regime. This worked well to begin with. While I got the sheep out of the shed, Ellen stood by the gate to turn them into the handling unit. Without any previous experience of sheep, Ellen was not terribly effective at moving the ewes, who were being their usual stubborn selves, but between us we ran them through the footbath and I separated those with a blue spot on their shoulder, scanned carrying a single, from those with no marks who'd be producing doubles.

As we completed this task Aub drove back into the yard, having just taken the dogs home. He offered to let the next pen of sheep out to join the selections. Thinking Ellen would get through the gates quicker than me, with my wonky leg, I sent her to turn the sheep into the handling unit again. Typically, the ewes were keen to come out on a bright sunny day, and with Ellen struggling to understand how I'd secured the last gate, ran straight past her and on towards Miserden, Aub in hot pursuit. He eventually turned them, leaving Ellen to stand the other side of the gateway to send them into the handling unit again. I stationed myself by the grain store, another escape route they often favour. Not so today, they opted for the footpath track behind the buildings. Rapidly fencing off the grain store escape route with hurdles, I rushed round to help Aub. He'd managed to get them back, only for them to make another dash for the village. Running faster than usual, anger screaming from his face, I let him round them up again while I blocked all escape routes and, eventually, we had them installed in the handling unit and sorted with the others.

It's amazing how a sunny day can affect a sheep's brain. You do realise how useless you are without the dogs.

Aub was on the phone, "I'll have to go, the feed lorry's arrived at Edgeworth."

He drove off to Edgeworth at great speed, and was still scowling when he returned. Although Ellen had planned to stay longer, I suggested she rang her mother to pick her up as soon as possible; there really wasn't anything else I could show her at the moment. I really felt her mother was more enthusiastic on her behalf than Ellen herself.

At least she was welcome to see how things were progressing in the lambing department at the end of the following week, when hopefully there should be some lambs on the ground.

END OF FEBRUARY

Why is it that February seems to last a whole year? That's what it feels like anyway. It seems to go on and on. Perhaps it's because we're waiting for lambing to start. Or perhaps it's the foul weather with yet more cold rain lashing down. No one even dreamed of trying to escape to the field today. Ok, so it was probably a good ten degrees warmer than last week, but spring was definitely not on its way yet.

Not a good day for the pigs either, well three of them anyway. The start of Bisley Lane Pork was happening this week. The candidates were three of the boys – sadly two were Bacon and Sausage who had grown into monsters – lucky Chorizo had a reprieve and was being kept as a boar for the Supercars because we all loved his orange colouring. The third candidate was one of the bought-in weaners. Not the one Mark had selected to go as he and Aub couldn't catch him when they were loading them at Edgeworth, but a fair specimen all the same.

We are so fortunate that all our meat animals have a very short journey to the local abattoir, as carefully driven those ten miles as they are looked after throughout their lives. The abattoir has a great reputation and we have no concerns about the handling of the animals, which are dispatched rapidly on arrival.

Then the relief after all that waiting. Two Blues lambed and this definitely gave me confidence that I hadn't got the dates completely wrong. Aub had already penned the first when I arrived at the farm. She was a ewe I'd thought would lamb in the next cycle, so I had got that wrong. She'd also had a bad foot for a while. When she didn't respond to antibiotics, I guessed it could be a thorn. Once penned Aub examined her to discover I was right. I gave her pen and strep and a shot of painkiller as she was obviously in discomfort, trying to lie down the whole time, on both lambs if possible. The stronger first born lamb was coping with suckling, but I fed the other one with colostrum. As soon as the ewe saw a bottle she got quite excited. Obviously a bottle lamb herself, with no built-in mothering instinct.

The second ewe lambed just after we'd fed. Due to have triplets, she produced a good ewe lamb but then appeared to have cleansing hanging down. On investigation she was very much like our early quad, with smelly afterbirth tangled up with the other two lambs, both sadly dead. Not a great result but mother and remaining child fine, so again, antibiotics to both ewe and lamb to avoid infection. I moved them to a lambing pen, just in time to realise that the ewe in pen one was sitting down with no lambs visible. Rapidly poking her so she stood up I retrieved two slightly squashed children and put them on the opposite side of the pen, one finding it hard to stand. Dopey woman. During the day I rescued her lambs a further twice, before putting them in the warm box. It was incredibly mild, but the poorly lamb had turned cold. Both needed removing or the ewe would only accept the one that stayed with her. Finally we decided to bottle the lambs. Aub had milked the ewe; it was too risky to leave them with her all night. In fairness to the ewe, her foot was very sore.

"Shut up talking and suck," I said to the lamb on my lap, trying to persuade it a bottle was just as good as its mother's teat. "It's not my fault your mother's trying to smother you. I'm trying to keep you alive."

So two lambs spent the night in the sitting room as puppy in the kitchen would have barked every time they moved. Twelve hours into lambing and I'm already covered in lamb poo and iodine. Both survived the night, but it was obvious the poorly one had been badly damaged. She was put back in the warm box, but didn't make it. The better lamb was returned to her mother, who was delighted and we kept a close eye to make sure she didn't sit on it again.

The outside lights that come on automatically when we cross the yard had failed, but as ever we were able to source more from Amazon. Aub fitted one outside the bike shed, which was great, but unfortunately we then couldn't switch the bike shed lights off. Looked like Aub's career move to electrician was on hold for the moment.

This year, we decided to have a full team to help with the lambing. How wonderful. I don't think we'd ever had full staff for lambing before. With my knee problems, and the fact I'd been saying for the last five years that I can't catch anything if it's having difficulty lambing, we now had a group of experienced lambers. Sadly we were missing Becca, who had a small baby taking priority, but the addition of Simon who was doing the night shift was great. The last team member, Ben, knew little about sheep, but he was as ever a great asset bedding up and helping to move ewes and lambs around.

Mark T, Aub and Ben were already at the farm, and Simon would be on duty overnight from eight pm through to six am, unless nothing was happening in the early hours, when he might go earlier.

Yesterday morning I was on Radio Gloucestershire chatting to Nicky Price about Jumping Over Clouds which was great fun. I'm used to Zoom meetings now, but strange doing it without video, for a radio show. At the end she asked me my thoughts on a new App, where farmers can record and judge their animals' emotions. I asked if I could be sceptical before going on air, but really, do we need an app to tell us if our animals are happy?

A good example of knowing our animals' behaviour was a ewe having triplets. She had shown a waterbag and Aub was monitoring her when I arrived at the yard to feed. He then went to feed outside, she was obviously waiting for breakfast before producing her lambs. This is typical of the ewes, especially Texels, who prioritise food above everything else. Not long after her nuts and haylage she found herself a corner of the shed and gave birth. I didn't need an App to tell me she was quite content with the situation, had made her own decision and would do what we expected.

As I explained to Nicky, no farmer likes their animals to be discontent. Unhappy animals don't thrive. We always try to make sure that groups of sheep remain together, as friendships and bonds are made. Should we have to separate any, we endeavour to keep friends together, and sheep can be most vocal when telling us we've taken away their friend, something we try to rectify. But it's common sense, not something technology can improve. I did feel it was one of those situations where money was available for sponsoring something and an App is the 'in' thing these days.

I printed out a sheet for all lambing staff with health and safety in mind, with emergency numbers and lambing protocols. One thing I stressed was that multiples or problem ewes were to be housed in the front pens, the back of the grain store is quite dark so problems can be missed. Mark T just announced that he'd put the set of triplets right at the back because the pens were a bit bigger there. All the pens are made up with two six foot and two four foot hurdles. I'm searching for the logic, but hey ho, things could only improve.

With additional staff, the only time we were on our own was from 5pm until 8pm. Just before Mark T left for the evening, he and Aub investigated a Blue ewe who seemed to be having problems. Definitely. Carrying triplets, the first was coming tail first. When this happens the cervix doesn't open up correctly as there is nothing to push against it as there is with correct presentation of front legs and head.

All was not well. Aub could barely get one finger inside her and the mucous surrounding the lambs smelt foul. They had to be dead, but also had to be removed, not the easiest of jobs. She was given the drug that should assist with opening her up, but after twenty minutes or so little had improved. I rang the vets. Paul would be with us in thirty minutes. Mark T went home and I held the fort as another ewe was lambing, while Aub drove back to the house to collect the caravan for Simon. The previous night he'd only had one ewe lamb and sitting in the milk shed can't be the warmest place in the middle of the night.

Paul eventually extricated all three lambs from the

Blue ewe, but with great difficulty as even with plenty of slipjel her poor insides were so dry. Not the most enjoyable experience for her, but the only option. A caesarean was far too risky with the lambs being dead and infection so easy to pass to her. Pumped with antibiotics and painkiller it was fingers crossed that she would recover. No worries about any infection through the flock, just malpresentation which may have killed the first a couple of days ago, toxins killing the others, but impossible to diagnose until she showed some discomfort.

Luckily, by the time we'd finished Simon had arrived for the night shift. I showed him the latest lambs, some needing colostrum as their mothers weren't letting milk down yet and others that needed keeping an eye on.

Being self-employed, our days usually never end if problems like this arise. It was a great relief to hand over to someone reliable.

On the other hand, while I appreciated having so much help during this first manic lambing week of the year, I do sometimes wonder if I've completely lost the knack of giving instructions, or if some people simply don't listen. After the ewes let themselves out of the far pen of the sheep shed, I asked Ben to tie the gate up. When I returned to check, the complication of the knot may well have secured his yacht in Monaco, but should Simon have tried to enter late at night in the dark I think he'd have broken his neck. Not only complex, but secured at ground level!

Feeding rams in the snow

Ready for tobogganing: Mark, Kate, three
children and small dog, all on the quad

MARCH

However the saying goes about March to do with lambs and lions, this year it definitely came in like a polar bear. The temperature dropped by a good ten degrees. A few brave snowdrops were making one last flourish in the wooded area approaching the farm and daffodils were starting to appear, although it would be a couple of weeks before those chose to flower. As we progressed through the month the crisp cold air changed to fog most mornings, though the temperature was slow to rise. Where had all our sunshine gone?

I found one of my smaller Blue lambs, in the warm milk machine pen, had caught his ear tag in the metal mesh of the door and was lying prostrate, cold and alone. I put him straight into the warm box, praying he'd survive but not very hopeful, though later he had sufficient suck to take a little milk. Later I tubed him to ensure he had a full stomach for the night and put him back with his friends, settled under the heat lamp. Amazingly, the following morning he was bright as a button, warm with a full tummy. Such a relief. Dramas like this often wake me through the night. Perhaps everyone who deals with animals feels the same.

Most of the ewes and lambs were still in at night and frolicking in the fields in the day. Troughs and hayracks were all set up in the shed, which makes life easier. Now our lambing staff had moved on to other flocks I was the first on the farm in the morning.

This is usually prior to dawn, night time still settled like a dark mantel over the farm. A few lights in the sheds make it easy to check the still pregnant ewes and those in pens with lambs. It's time to refill clean water buckets, offer handfuls of hay and enjoy the murmuring of ewes chatting to their lambs. Any freshly lambed are congratulated on doing the job well by themselves. It's a delight to find a ewe with two polished lambs standing beside her, stomachs full and contentment reigning. These are slipped into a clean individual pen to bond for the next twenty-four hours. The worst scenario is either a ewe with just the swollen head of her lamb and possibly one leg hanging out, or four ewes all eating contentedly at the hayrack, as Texels are wont to do, with an assortment of unclaimed lambs running round the shed.

Gradually darkness becomes day. The process might go unnoticed when I'm busy, if not for the dawn chorus.

Thrush, blackbird, robin, wren and many others join in this beautifully orchestrated musical drama. For five minutes, or is it ten, the strong, dominant whistling is so loud it often has me looking to see who's arrived in the yard. Then it's passed. The daytime birdsong has none of the strength and determination of the morning alert.

At breakfast time, the noise in the shed reaches a crescendo, as everyone demands to be fed first. Going through the main pens to feed a couple of recently lambed ewes penned at the back feels like swimming with great white sharks (not that I've experienced this, but can imagine it's very similar). Texels are totally unforgiving when food is about and I often wonder if I'll stay upright. As I empty the bucket down the last feeder all goes quiet. Once again I hear birdsong: the great tit marking his territory with his repetitive call, against an indignant robin.

Now is the time I walk through all the pens, checking on the lambs. Taking time to stop and look is vital. Anything looking unhappy stands out from those skipping up and down, enjoying the space left by their mothers crowding into the troughs. It's always harder work the week after lambing when we're on our own.

Thankfully, this week, Mark T could still work for an hour for several mornings, mainly to help us turn different lots out for the first time.

How is it when the distance from the sheep shed

to the field is no more than 5 metres, several ewes who left the shed with two lambs in tow, lost them by the time they reached the gate. At the sight of grass, even if it wasn't the most exciting amount, they turned into racehorses and I'd be left with 5 or 6 lambs to mother-up. I don't open the field gate until everyone has arrived with said lambs alongside, but every year it still happens. Doubles were worse than singles, if they had one lamb they were happy.

Singles were different. The ewes spent so much time frenetically circling their only lamb, it often reached the field before they have, at which point they decide they must have left it in the shed, turn like a quarter-horse and leg it back to the fortunately closed door. With everyone happily reconnected in the field, it had to be coffee time.

This continued for the first three or four days of going to this field. On day five they decided they needed a change of field and if the dogs and I weren't quick enough, they would have run straight past the gateway, heading for something they hope will be better. Every year, like clockwork, they do this. This is usually when they find themselves staying out 24/7 ...

One late ewe gave birth with difficulty. A huge lamb, grown bigger because his mother had hung on so long and eaten too much, but it's amazing how spirits rise when a lamb who struggles to be born because of his size immediately breathes and gives the appearance of a show winner.

These days, I'm noticing my age a little more. I'm loath to admit it but Mark T manages to fly round the yard feeding and watering in a fraction of the time it takes me. Oh, the joys of youth. We'd finished tagging the last few lambs, putting families out in bigger pens now. With Mark's help, my contribution is noting down the tag numbers and weights, but I still feel totally drained. It's been a hard couple of weeks. Once back home for coffee, after Aub had gone to North Farm to feed the others, I sat in a chair and dozed off. Everything else could be done later. There's only so much the body can cope with and by the evening I certainly needed a glass of wine. My biggest calamity of the day was finding it impossible to unscrew the bottle top. Thank goodness I studied physics. Running the screw top under hot water until it expanded slightly. What a relief.

Both Maisie and Jilly were due to have their annual vaccines, but I'd already changed Jilly's appointment to a vet check-up. Her constant desire to stay in bed until late afternoon was worrying me. Part of me was sure it was simply general stiffness and old age, and cold wet mornings offered little appeal to anyone, but felt she needed checking. Katy, her vet, decided on a regular dose of Loxicom to alleviate arthritic pain, but also took some bloods to see if anything else was causing a problem.

Crocuses, primroses and trees were in full blossom at the bottom of Birdlip hill as I drove to the vets. It often seems like a totally different world down there, compared to the one we know.

There was less work to do with all ewes and lambs out in the daytime, but with horrendous weather forecast it would be silly to put them out full time when we had room in the barns for them to come in at nights. Not only easier to feed in the sheds, but satisfying to know they were inside as damaging winds howled all night. With a couple still to lamb I checked the cameras at 5.30 am, but realised it had frozen at 4.30 and was now not working. I wasn't in too much of a panic because nothing untoward was happening at 4.30, but I drove to the farm just after six.

A large tree was down across the gateway to the Blues' field – obviously my brain was in neutral as I didn't realise this was why we had no electricity. Everything not battened down had blown across the yard, including Aub's ton bag of plastic containers. Might push him to dispose of them. Might not.

Luckily there was enough warm water in the heater to mix milk for the machine lambs. The lack of a heat lamp was not a problem as by now they were well grown, but one small Blue lamb was studying it, as though enquiring why it wasn't on. Thankfully Western Power were very efficient, although it took them half a day to mend the broken wires caused by the tree.

A trip to Cirencester market was planned for our son

Mark to buy more pigs. His own home bred animals were now mainly sausages and bacon, and, while more were in the pipeline, some weaners were needed to keep up the supply. I opted to join Aub and Mark as I hadn't been anywhere for so long. As usual, we were running late and the trip was fraught with problems – trees down, loose polo ponies and a fuel lorry stuck in the way; eventually we arrived.

Pigs are only sold once a month at our local market, so there were a fair number in. Mark wanted ones reared outdoors, as these were destined for the woods at Bisley Lane. Pigs seemed very popular this month and the Gloucester/Pietrain were selling for so much money. After much discussion, Mark homed in on some outdoor reared Berkshire crosses, pretty black piglets with a narrow white stripe down the nose and white feet, which were brought home successfully. Hopefully they would later produce pork of a similar quality to the Pietrain/Old Spot crosses.

The results came back from Jilly's blood tests suggesting she might have a metabolic problem and two weeks of tablets were prescribed.

Dear old 1105 died. I had great affection for this Blue Texel ewe. Everyone thinks that farmers don't get attached to their ageing animals. This isn't the case at all. Silly old girl had had two lambs, one of which I'd taken off her immediately and hand reared as there was no way she'd cope with both, but she'd been doing the other one so well. It's sad when one of the golden oldies has tried so hard to do her bit. I'll really miss her. Thankfully her lamb sensibly drank once moved into the bottle department, as he was only two weeks old.

1105 was born in 2013, one of three super ewes we bred that year by a homebred ram, Taro. He was by a Pen Y Bec sire, bred by Glynn Arrowsmith, who came un-named, but took on the mantle of Arrow. The other two by Taro, were 1101 and 1103. Numbers may not seem like names, but I can assure you they mean as much to us. These three ewes won at major shows, including Championships and produced some of the best Blue Texel offspring we have had.

Dear old Arrow also caused a major drama when we decided to sell him. With only a small flock at the time, we'd retained a number of his daughters and needed to replace him with a different bloodline. He was a superb ram, worthy of a chance in another pedigree flock. At the Worcester sale I almost withdrew him, he was such a lovely sheep and had done us so well, but another breeder we knew was very keen to purchase him. Feeling a lump in my throat when he was loaded on to his trailer, I knew we'd made a sensible decision and he'd gone to a very good home. We also needed the finance to replace him in a few weeks' time.

The lump in the throat turned to tears later that evening when his new owner rang me to ask if he'd been unwell, as he certainly was now. Horrified to discover Arrow could hardly move, I assured the buyer that he must get his vet out, at our expense, and we would refund his money and bring him home when possible. Another couple of very tense days followed before Arrow showed any signs of recovery. At least his purchaser was now sure it was nothing we'd known about at the sale. In fact, although the vets couldn't be certain, they felt he'd had an anaphylactic reaction from a sting on arrival at his new home. The outcome was that he stayed with his new owner, who has been delighted with his offspring. Aubrey did say if I was going to spend three days in tears every time I sold one of the stock rams then perhaps it would be easier to keep them all, and I don't think we've sold one since, although a further mistake was selling Taro at the end of his shearling season, having only lightly used him, as the 1100 ewes proved so good!

Bottle lambs

With Leo and Maisie

MID MARCH

The end of home schooling was an occasion for celebration. It had been causing so many problems for families at this time. Not least Heather, who was trying to work full time while also sorting out 7-year-old Leo's education. As a family, we all tried to assist with Zoom. My contribution was helping with reading and creative writing a couple of mornings a week. This worked well to begin with, but later lacked success as concentration waned.

Heather would send me through the tasks his school had set for us to follow. Leo was great at making up brilliant stories, although when he showed me his writing it sometimes left a little to be desired. Still better than nothing, and his drawings were brilliant. Then, suddenly instead of seeing a studious face, often chewing his pencil, my screen would simply portray a pair of legs and feet resting on the back of settee.

"Leo, what are you doing?" I'd ask.

"Granny, I think I've done enough now."

Unfortunately, this might be only ten minutes into our half hour slot. I could sometimes solve the problem by suggesting we both continued with the paper his school had provided, reading a paragraph each. Sometimes he simply disappeared.

Being a teacher, Kate was having far greater success with Toby, Wilfred and Bluebell.

Mother's Day is an occasion our daughter Heather has always loved celebrating and even with lockdown she planned to deliver 'afternoon tea', including homemade (by her husband Kevin) scotch eggs and sausage rolls, delicious sandwiches and tiny cakes.

Like so many other mothers, I'd seen very little of her or her family recently – Zoom can only go so far. The plan was for Heather, Kevin and Leo to deliver tea early in the afternoon, when the sun would be shining and it would be warm enough for them to hand over the 'food parcel' and have a quick socially distanced chat over the garden wall. Sadly, at 2.15 that afternoon I was sitting in the milk shed at the farm waiting for the vet to do a caesarean. Heather, and family, already en route, said they'd leave the box of tea in the garage. Not enamoured with sheep farming, Heather does understand that emergencies happen, but had no desire to witness the operation.

The ewe in question shouldn't still have been here.

Marked as a cull, having contracted mastitis last year, she had somehow made her way to the breeding field rather than being sold. Still on the farm at scanning, we discovered she was carrying two lambs, so just accepted the situation.

As her due date approached she appeared to be growing larger and larger around the stomach area, with her useless udder reminiscent of 'Madonna with the big boobies'. We'd been hopeful she'd lamb at the same time as some others, when we might be able to adopt her lambs onto another ewe. No such luck. She'd hung on until everything else had lambed to produce her water bag on Mothers' Day.

Aub had examined her around 11am, as she wasn't showing any signs of lambing by herself, and realised she hadn't opened up at all, a good sign that a lamb is coming backwards, often tail first. Because a lamb isn't putting pressure on the birth canal with its front feet and nose, this causes discomfort, but does not alert the ewe's body that she's giving birth. We gave her medication that should have helped, but to no avail, which was why I anticipated Paul, our vet, any minute to take the lambs out of the side door.

An emergency at son Mark's farm meant I was still waiting for Aub when Paul arrived, so we started to build a makeshift operating table ourselves. Paul suggested putting a pallet on top of the bars of the walk-through feeder. I did query whether this might be a bit high for him, he's not that tall, but he assured me he would reach. Once Aub returned, all three of us struggled to lift the enormous ewe onto her high-rise operating table, and I found a feed bin for Paul to stand on!

Aub held her head; her feet were tied to the pallet to stop her escaping, while Paul operated. There is little comparison here to 'Call the Midwife'. Still aware of social distancing, Paul threw the lambs towards me, rather than handing them over, but luckily I caught them. I dried each one, clearing their airways of fluids and encouraged them to breathe.

The first lamb was big, but I had little time to deal with him before number two arrived, rapidly followed by number three. No wonder she'd looked enormous. I rubbed all three with towels and clean straw, then mixed some artificial colostrum and bottle fed them. By the time I'd finished, the ewe was being lowered to the ground; an easier job than getting her up there, and she was penned up with her contented children, able to lick them dry and clean. A successful, if expensive outcome.

We left her lambs with her until the following day, bottling them every four hours, but then moved them to the warm milk machine. I hate distressing a ewe by doing this, but I think she realised she couldn't cope. The lambs took to the machine immediately and settled in with the others. Their mother called to them a couple of times then settled down to eat hay with her friend. She was destined to enjoy a good final summer at grass.

Heather and I did manage to meet up for five minutes later that week in the agricultural merchant's car park (I needed more milk powder), when I again said how much we'd appreciated the delicious tea at supper time.

In our wintery heights, the first buds were just starting to show on the hawthorn hedges. Down in the valley, it looked like beautiful weather for Cheltenham, strange without its crowds, but still enjoyable to watch on TV, between sheep activities.

The second lot of ewes were just starting to lamb so, as usual, I tried to check those in the 18 acre as I walked down the 9 acre. But this morning I got a bollocking for not noticing a ewe had lambed in the field. Just possible it hadn't lambed when I'd walked down the adjacent field, or I simply didn't see. My distance eyesight isn't brilliant without glasses and at certain places the hedge is higher than me anyway. I think Aub was cross was because I'd noticed the small stretch of electric fence by the footpath was down when he hadn't. This had been fairly obvious as the footpath was covered in sheep's doobies, showing there had been a minor escape, but I didn't bother to emphasise this.

The ewe, having had the one lamb, looked as though she was having problems with the second, but proved particularly awkward to be caught, so no real improvement in Aub's temper when he brought her in. This didn't get any better when she decided not to follow her first lamb and I couldn't stop her running past me to make a circuit of the yard. Eventually we contained her and Aub assisted, as the second lamb was coming backwards. On its arrival into this world, it had no desire to breathe. I'd shown initiative by fetching the lambing bucket, with the wonder implement for draining fluid from lambs' lungs, often a life saver when they come backwards. Even so, his enthusiasm was definitely lacking. After several attempts of massaging him, tickling his nose with straw, which did result in a sneeze then nothing more, this lamb looked as though he'd prefer to doze off rather than gather himself up and live.

As a last resort Aub decided to swing him, something farmers always used to do to remove any phlegm and mucous from a lamb that's come backwards or simply refusing to breathe. It can work, but can also damage them, so it's a last resort. Moving out into the alleyway outside the pens, Aub held him securely by the back legs and swung him backwards and forwards several times, then dropped him back on the straw. The lamb gave a big gulp and baa'd. Thank goodness. With a further piece of straw up his nose and a couple more sneezes it looked as though he'd got the hang of breathing and I promised him it would become habit forming after a while.

Our farm has a lovely atmosphere. I've often done

the late night check during lambing and it always feels a safe and happy place. On quiet, cloudless nights the sky can be filled with stars, light pollution from Gloucester and Cheltenham not quite reaching our hilltop. Other times, the elements make the yard a battlefield, the wind, rain and sometimes snow being driven by freezing winds. Buckets, plastic and anything not permanently held down crashing across the yard. Devastation to be cleared up the following day.

It's not really my usual shift, but if Aub is asleep in front of the fire and I'm awake, I'll grit my teeth and drive up to the farm, leaving his mobile on the arm of the chair, making sure mine's in my pocket. Any dire emergency and he'll have to join me, but if all is well, he can have a few more hours to recover from his day in the sheep shed.

This night, wrapped up well against the cold night air, I left Jilly sleeping in her kennel. Maisie was as usual insistent on joining me. Parking by the main sheep shed, where some of the lights were kept on overnight so our arrival didn't cause a major panic, I could easily check if all was well. Hopefully late at night all is calm.

The New Shed housed the expectant Blues who were imminent to give birth. All were happy and content, chewing cud or sleeping so it was on to the lambing pens, both in the grain store and the main shed, where the ewes were sure to need more hay and water. I woke all sleeping lambs, much to their annoyance, but I wanted to see them stretch and check they had full tummies, even if they glare at me. It's so easy to miss a lamb that hasn't fed by leaving it peacefully sleeping, thinking all is okay when it's really just weak from lack of milk. They would all have been checked earlier in the evening, but I always feel it's one of the most important things to be done late at night.

All was well in the pens and all looked quiet in the main sheds, so I did one more check, walking along the feeders, where I could get a better view of those at the back of the shed. This was where I caught sight of one I'd missed, easy to do as she was just in the first stages of labour, with just a waterbag showing. She could wait. One for Aub to check in an hour.

Back home I set the alarm on Aub's phone to wake him in an hour and left a note on the table saying which ewe had started. Then to bed. We'll grunt at each other again in the morning.

What bitter weather. I sometimes think our farmyard must be the coldest place on earth, when the east wind blows. Wrapped up in a thick jacket it almost felt like I was just wearing a bra and pants, perish the thought! It's horrible knowing young lambs are out in the fields in this. I know they have full tummies and will be fine, it's simply cold, not wet – and when checked in the morning they were all skipping around oblivious of my worries, thank goodness.

This bitter cold is the hardest to cope with – once everything becomes frozen the workload trebles. Even down to the effort of closing all the shed doors behind you, although you'll be back there in no time. Just a few minutes of cold wind can freeze the taps and pipes again.

When I turned Clemmie out this morning, wrapped up to the eyeballs in equine duvets, she ignored the slice of hay I'd put by the gate. Her attention was taken by two crows, social distancing, staring at each other in the middle of the field. At least, I think they were crows. I didn't have my glasses on. They could have been penguins, judging by the temperature.

Aub was happy this morning: a Blue had triplets alongside a white Texel with a single, the Texel stole one of the blue lambs and adopted it, which made life much easier, as each ewe now had two to rear. Sadly, about two days later the white decided she only wanted the blue and kicked her own lamb off. Luckily, we saw what was happening and brought her and her family back into a pen, but it took over a week for the white lamb to look loved again. I then moved her to a stable where there was only one other ewe with a couple of lambs and she spent three days there before moving out into a field. All was now well, but sometimes sheep do the most unexplained things.

Toby's ewe gave birth to two lovely lambs, one of each, although the ram lamb was far bigger than the ewe lamb, who had additional colostrum to ensure it wasn't all drunk by her huge brother. Both were beautiful lambs and Toby was delighted when he came to visit that evening. While Mark helped Aub and me feed and hay the sheep indoors, Toby just sat in his ewe's pen stroking his lambs. I think he'd have stayed there all night if we'd let him.

At the end of March, the clocks leapt forward an hour and the weather improved. Luckily the livestock was unaware of the time change – we didn't catch up with it until later in the day. It was actually quite nice to go to bed at 8.30pm instead of 9.30pm when I'd been on the early shift.

What did surprise me was the realisation that it was back to being dark at 6am. But it was lovely to be in the yard when the dawn chorus woke the natural world once again.

Jess was still sleeping in her cage in the kitchen, and having done the late run with Aub had no desire to be woken up at six. She lay curled up in her now chewed bed, one paw over her nose, eyes shut and the definite 'go away' message emanating from the area.

I usually make a cup of tea after I check the sheep on the cameras, before heading to the farm to feed the endless number of animals, unless I see a shed full of new lambs and feel I should rush up immediately. As I revolved the camera it made a slight whirring sound that attracted the sheep's attention. It was funny to come face to face with a sheep watching me watching her.

Checking the ewes and lambs out in the small

paddock by the sheds we soon discovered Toby's ewe had decided she only liked the ewe lamb, so we brought her back into a small pen, hoping she might mother-up both of them.

Toby and Wilfred ready for night lambing

APRIL LAMBING

It's always lovely to go up to the farm in the morning to find nothing has lambed and all is well with those born the previous day. We tagged a number of lambs in the pens, but were amazed when a blue ewe, who had been penned with her lamb for 48 hours, once turned in the big pen was frightened of her lamb now it was wearing a pink tag. It took her about half an hour to accept this was her own she'd been living with for two days, her temperament alternating between fear and anger at the lamb. Then, just as suddenly as she'd taken a dislike to it, she settled down to eat hay and let it suck. We find something new every year!

Toby's ewe was still disliking her ram lamb, so as a last resort she was put in the adopter, where both lambs could feed but she couldn't see them. Of all the sheep to have a problem, why did it have to be Toby's?

It was trying to snow again. There were a few fat flakes drifting round the yard, looking for somewhere cold to settle. Shouldn't be difficult. An atmospheric landscape for a trip to a funeral. An old friend Andrew, who with wife Sylvia, started keeping Blue Texels at the same time as we did, had tragically died. His health had never been good in all the time we'd known him, mainly suffering from heart problems. I was going to miss him.

I've had many great days out with Andrew at Blue Texel meetings and other events, being on the committee when Andrew was Chairman of the Society. He'd been a breath of fresh air, when so many in his position, both before and after him, had moulded the Society to suit their purpose. He'd simply worked for the good of the breed.

This had to be the first time I'd ventured out during the Covid pandemic, but the virus was causing me less problems than my wardrobe. What should I wear? What could I get into? Amazing how pairs of smart trousers seem to have shrunk while loitering in a drawer or hanging in the wardrobe. Eventually I found a wonderful pair of fawn trousers that have seen me through all sorts of occasions and, miraculously, still fitted.

Andrew's funeral was no sombre occasion, nor would he have wanted it to be. A number of us had written amusing pieces about our memories, and not being a religious man, the musical offerings were the theme from Star Wars, one of his favourite series, and 'Combine Harvester' by the Wurzels …

I somehow managed to be up before the heating came on and it was cold. Great weather for lockdown to be eased for pubs to re-open outdoors!

Rarely have I felt less inspired to put on my outdoor clothing and venture up to the farm, but by 6.30am I couldn't put it off any longer. There were still twelve lambs waiting for their bottles. And then a little Blue gimmer gave us a lovely surprise ewe lamb out in the field. Why a surprise? Mainly because Aub went through those still to lamb last week and only kept three in the shed that looked imminent. One lambed that evening, the others were still intact! So much for the master shepherd.

A second visit to the vets for Jill, where Katy agreed the new tablets had done nothing, simply making her sleepy, so to discontinue them, but that Jill should stay on the Loxicom. As light relief Jess was constantly underfoot at the yard. If I lost sight of her for a moment I knew I'd find her looking under a gate, sheep watching. Although still unorthodox in her style, her enthusiasm is never doubted.

For our grandchildren, a major highlight of the Easter holidays is night lambing with Grandpa – although even he cannot cope with all four children there at one time. Farm safety needs to be observed at all times, and while the three boys can form a great team during the day, night lambing is limited to two at most, and at only three years old Bluebell has not yet joined the team. By Easter the weather is rarely as bitterly cold as it is for February lambing, and with less sheep to lamb, tensions are not so high.

The fun element actually starts when Grandpa takes the old caravan up to the farm, checking the electrical connections still work, and makes the internal arrangements into a large double bed. This may already be in place in February, but the weekend of its arrival is always part of their fun, in anticipation of the later lambing.

When the lambing sleepover happens, Wilfred is usually in charge of the 'goodies box'. This consists of all types of chocolate bars for the boys and Kate usually includes Aub's favourite flapjacks. The chocolate bars are counted regularly and sometimes quality checked by Wilf and Leo, if he is joining the team, while Toby has been known to confiscate, saying they're for midnight feasts not mid afternoon snacks.

Lambing obviously goes on 24/7, but not with quite so much pressure as the early flock. I leave Aub administrating over evening feeds and checks, while small boys rush round topping up water buckets and filling hayracks. Initially they need a little direction, although Toby, now eleven, is so knowledgeable he can usually sort out any problems. The art is to do so without an argument. Any lambs needing bottles are fed with enthusiasm, their beds tidied, and if old enough their troughs are filled with pellets.

Aub will then check all is quiet and content, walking along the lambing pens and the sheep shed, his little entourage following, noticing things he might not. Once happy all is well, they return to the house for supper before returning for the main night shift.

The boys are noticeably keener to get back to the farm than their grandfather is. After supper, once settled in his armchair, possibly in front of a log fire, it takes a lot to move him. The boys and I will watch the cameras, but at the suspicion of someone needing attention Aub is forced into the night time ritual. I usually tidy up, then go to bed. Mine is the early shift when I often find the night staff all sound asleep in the caravan.

If the evening is cold, the first thing Aub does is switch the electric heater on in the caravan. Then he'll instruct the boys to go quietly along the walk-through feeders, where the pregnant ewes can be checked for signs of discomfort or lambing without stressing them. Nothing may be happening, but if it is, Toby will usually be the first to notice a problem. If anyone has lambed before they arrive, the lambs will have their navels sprayed with iodine, sometimes very liberally (the boys trying to clean stained fingers the following day) and carried round to the pens. Aub makes sure the ewe is following and ensures the gate to the sheep shed is closed securely. There have been times when this has been left to a child, only to find a yard full of ewes wandering about when they return from the penning department.

Everyone receives fresh hay and water and any bottle lambs have their late feed before the boys inform Grandpa that it must be time for feasts. Having directed them to thoroughly wash their hands in the milk shed, and secured a strong cup of coffee for himself, they all creep into the caravan, lit by the tiny wall light that still works. The goodie box is soon dealt with and Wilfred usually retires for the night, although Toby may still help with the two o'clock check.

On my early run, I look round then check all is well in the caravan. If I need assistance I will wake Aub, and Toby may stir, otherwise I leave them for another couple of hours. The boys will be full of the night's adventures and Aub will just be looking forward to catching up on some sleep in the armchair during the afternoon.

Why do farmers always have days like today? Last night Aub found a lovely Texel ram lamb completely prostrate in the field. He first thought it was just sleeping in the evening sun, but soon realised it wasn't well. Its mother was full of milk and the lamb certainly didn't look as though he lacked food, but something was definitely wrong. After ten minutes of trying to catch up his mother and twin, I pointed out that this lamb didn't look as though it was going to make the night, and certainly wouldn't be put in a pen with its mother, so we left her and the twin in the field. Giving painkillers and antibiotics, although having no idea what we were treating really, we made him comfortable in a bed alongside the bottle lambs, where he wouldn't feel alone, but couldn't be touched by them. Sadly, the next morning I found him dead. Not a surprise really, a twisted gut being the most likely cause.

What did come as a surprise was finding the lamb in the adjacent stable dead as well. Her mother had kicked her off when another lamb had got mismothered and tried to suck from her. We'd sorted them out fairly rapidly, penning both ewes with their lambs in different buildings, and this ewe seemed to have got it together with her own lamb, but she may have trodden on it, something Texels are quite prone to doing, even in a six foot square pen. The final straw came when Aub fed the lambs at lunchtime, only to find the Blue Texel ewe lamb whose mother had abandoned it a couple of weeks ago, had also died. I'd tried, unsuccessfully to persuade her to suck a bottle and tubed her for several days, then decided she was old enough to wean onto course mix and water. Sadly, this was not to be.

It's heartbreaking putting so much time and effort into these problem lambs, for them not to survive. It was a nice relief to take a ride round the fields and see all the success stories where mothers are raising their lambs like normal sheep should. Thankfully all the lambs on the machine seemed to be coping, though one Lleyn ewe who was struggling with two lambs, was now struggling with the one I've left on her, so this might also end up in the machine department.

Facebook reminded me that it was about a year ago we sold our black and white cobs. They were an experience! Having decided to stop breeding horses, I faltered when I was left with one last youngster on the farm. I must have had withdrawal symptoms. Either that or my dealing blood overcame me. When I discovered the Juddmonte stud had two remaining black and white foals, I couldn't resist going to look.

A few years ago, not content with the horses we were breeding, I'd purchased some additional foals. Firstly from the Godolphin stud at Newmarket, then a couple of years later from the local Juddmonte stud, both who kept a number of cobby type mares whose foals would be artificially reared if a thoroughbred foal lost its mother and needed a surrogate mare.

Our first venture from the Juddmonte brought us two of the last remaining foals that year, out of these cobby mares by a thoroughbred stallion, bred to event. Looking at the foals that were left, most having already been sold, we liked a small dark brown filly and I picked a bigger grey colt. Sadly, on inspection, and warning from the stud manager, we found a deformity in the colt's mouth, the reason he was still there, but were directed towards another big colt, liver chestnut going grey.

"God, he's ugly," Aub muttered. "Let's just take the

little one." She'd been his selection from the start, but not really wanting to take one on its own, and possibly getting a better deal taking the two, I chose to take the colt as well.

"He'll never look as ugly again as he does today," I assured Aub on the way home. "He's well put together apart from his head being too big for him and having no neck."

"Hmm. A good description."

I photographed our new purchases when they arrived at home. Never once did I doubt my decision, and my ugly duckling proved me right. He is now a much-prized dappled grey hunter enjoying life with a family in Germany. Aub's little filly also excelled herself. Not growing to the 15.2hh I expected, but staying at 14.2hh, she is a top class event pony, also living happily with a lovely family, still in England. I think the stallion who fathered them passed on his jumping ability and lovely temperament to both.

Having got the bug, I wanted more Juddmonte foals. By now the TB stallion was not being used, but a very compact coloured cob stallion was the sire of the present crop of foals available. I was disappointed as they really weren't the type of horses I was used to having, but they were cheaper than buying a calf and the whole idea was to run them on until three year olds and sell, unbroken. Coloured horses of all types were in demand and one of the foals was quite striking.

He'd been unwell when the first foals were sold, so

hadn't looked good or been selected, but he appeared to have made a full recovery and I was hooked. His companion didn't impress me, but was a good workmanlike sort, so they both returned to the farm. Sadly, neither had been very well handled, unlike the original foals we had bought, so the nightmare began.

Cowboy, the smart one, and Indian were established in the stables, where Aub and I played with and handled them for a number of days before leading them out to the front field. I was aiming to bring them in each night to get them used to the regime and more handling. Each leading one, as we turned the corner out of the yard towards the field, the colts leant away from us, with necks like bullocks, my pony pulling me over and Aub just managing to keep hold of his. With mine re-captured we managed, somehow, to turn them round in the field so they were facing us before slipping the ropes from their headcollars and that was the last contact we had with them for several days!

Experienced friends came up with all sorts of ideas, the best one being to castrate them immediately as we felt testosterone was partly to blame for their behaviour, but this was late in the year. The ground being so wet and muddy as November approached, our vet advised against doing this in case of infection, suggesting we left them colts for the winter. It was decided we would herd them into the quarry field, where there was a field shelter and they could stay, unhandled, until the following spring. Hopefully we would then be in a position to herd them into the yard and the stables for castration.

Although sometimes fraught, in fairness their lives continued quite happily. Feed and hay was delivered daily and we were soon able to stroke them at feed times, although they could still show their wild side.

Castration, an excitement on its own, did make them more handleable and they had their feet trimmed on a regular basis. We elected to bring them in to the stables twice a year, for four or five days so we could deal with their management, and gradually handling them did become easier. While I don't consider myself easily stressed, I did regret my purchase, and after Aub continued to moan about them I generously gave them to him. He immediately took a much greater interest in them and life became easier. When we sold them, the money would still be ours!

Selling them became a real eye opener. Both had been born in early February, so their mothers were available to take on thoroughbred foals, if necessary, who would have been born at the same time. April of their third year I decided to advertise them on Facebook. By now they had grown into strong, 15 hand plus horses. Good straight movers, ideal for both riding and driving. I selected a price I could happily go down from, as they hadn't cost us much to rear, but was amazed at how many people wanted to buy them.

I hadn't really placed an advert, more a suggestion that they were looking for new homes. Cowboy was priced higher than Indian, but he was such a looker he was the one most people were after. A woman contacted me, wishing to come and see Cowboy and I delayed her for a few days as we were busy sorting sheep. Then someone I've known for a long time rang to ask if both ponies were available. This made life a little difficult, but I felt it would be an ideal home as I knew Abby was quite capable of breaking and bringing on both, but didn't want to be unfair to the first woman. Looking her up on Facebook I realised we had a mutual friend, whom I phoned to ask about the suitability of the prospective buyer. The resulting answer was convincing and I offered the two ponies to Abby, who, with experienced assistance quietly loaded both into a trailer the following day, and has been delighted with them ever since.

Not so the other lady. When I explained my decision was purely made for the animal's benefit, realising she probably had little idea of what she might be taking on, she was furious. She threw such a tantrum, accusing me of defrauding her and threatening all sorts of action. I apologised, but assured her I felt both ponies were better going together to the same experienced home. It materialised she was looking for something for her boyfriend to ride, and a few months later she bought him something that put him in hospital. I feel Cowboy could have done that quite promptly too!

Cowboy and Indian

Jess always takes the prime
seat in the gator

MID APRIL

D o I always decide I hate sheep about the middle of April? Especially those that can't rear their lambs. As I pointed out to a small Lleyn x lamb sitting on my lap, blatantly refusing to suck a bottle teat, 'it's no good your mother rashly producing four lambs if she seems incapable of rearing any of you'. Whatever I said made little impression as I ended up tubing her to ensure she made it through the night.

This was the final one of quads on the Lleyn ewe in question. I'd already had to rescue three of the lambs from her, but I'd imagined that being a lovely caring sheep she would rear the remaining one with love and kindness, but my idea was severely thwarted when her teats swelled to the size of a cow's and the little lamb couldn't cope. Hence this also ended up in the bottle department. Christened Baby, she was taking such a small amount from a bottle that she was still being tubed at night, but I was hoping things would improve. Their mother was enjoying herself out at grass, with a big red line denoting her cull status down her back.

On the plus side, most of my other lambs were looking good. The eight weaned ones were devouring creep and growing like weeds, and four more would join them at the weekend. They had a large section of the sheep shed at nights and a grass paddock to play in during the day, although they were usually ready to come back in by lunchtime.

There were now just seven lambs on a machine with ad lib creep, who would be changed onto bottles in two weeks' time, otherwise they over-indulge on ad lib milk and die. The Charolais crosses from the caesarean were doing well, bottled three times a day, and a fourth lamb in the same pen had now caught on to the skill of sucking for England, although he wouldn't drink from the bottle rack like the others. He needed the one-to-one treatment, me holding him and stroking his nose or he refused to drink.

As it had come a bit warmer I'd switched off their heat light and moved the smaller lambs to a bigger stable with a cosy area made of bales, which some slept on and others tucked in alongside. 'Red spot', another lamb rescued when her mother decided to stop feeding her, identified by a colour mark on her shoulder, was beginning to look a little more like a lamb than a praying mantis. And 'iodine eyebrow', who obviously had been marked by an over-zealous grandchild, the older Lleyn daughter, was also doing well on a bottle. I'd given up trying to make them suck the machine. I felt sure they'd grasp it at some point, but I'd rather have them looking well and growing on with regular bottle feeds, although it was incredibly time consuming.

Yet another beautiful spring morning brought a little light rain, but we needed it. I'm one of those people who like warm, soft rain between 10pm and 6am, but at that moment I'd have taken anything. The ground was like concrete and we had no grass. Combine that with the feed bill for an extra 4 tonne of ewe cake. One of the bonuses of the long dry spell was that I managed to purchase new wellies – the shelves were overflowing with them.

Jilly greatly improved now that she was simply on pain relief. Most mornings she came to the farm with me, so my car was becoming a dog travelling outfit, with Maisie and Jilly in the back and Jess straight into the front seat. I think I would struggle to have all of them in the dog compartment at the back, so didn't argue with her. Jill needed lifting in and out of the car, but really seemed to enjoy being back at the farm, in a supervisory position. If we're moving sheep around I make sure she doesn't get in the way, as Texels can be so unforgiving. She can't move quickly and even if she does it's usually in the wrong direction.

The Blue gimmers were sheared today and looking

good. I was really pleased with how they came out of their wool, and a pat on the back for Mark T who sheared them so well. Now all we needed was some good grass for them to grow into lovely sheep.

Aub caused a major drama though. Heading off with a load of fertilizer for fields between Cranham and Caudle Green, the tow bar of the trailer started to bend. (The trailer was well stacked, so it could possibly have had something to do with the amount he was carrying). When he rang me saying it had broken I had horrific visions of the trailer running backwards and squashing cars behind, but he'd realised the problem before it got to this stage. Luckily it happened close to cousin Martin's farm, who came to the rescue and unloaded the fertilizer with his JCB, just leaving a couple of bags right on the back to balance the trailer as Aub manoeuvred it off the road and into his field. With the fertilizer reloaded onto another trailer a major disaster was averted and the delivery continued. That just left the dead trailer to collect and take for repairs.

We'd been told some weeks ago that Worcester market were holding an early female sale, but had rather poo-pooed the idea, agreeing it was far earlier than we'd consider selling gimmers, and anyway they were still wearing their winter woollies. However, friends and other Blue Texel breeders, Giles and Sally, who had already entered some, talked us into entering two. I suppose the thought that people had not been out much, and were likely to have money burning a hole in their pockets made us realise we ought to just take something. I picked out two gimmers simply by their numbers rather than going to the field to select them, most of our February born lambs were well-grown and would fit the bill. We brought them in to find one had lost an ear tag, but a replacement was sought quickly and I was pleased with my 'selection'.

Having wintered out on top of the Cotswolds, the sheep did look rather woolly, but Kate, our trimmer, assured me she could make them look presentable, and certainly did. This didn't go without incident. On trimming day, Kate's vehicle broke down on the 417 just before the Air Balloon. She sent me a video of the traffic passing which looked horrific. The police had to cordon off one lane for the AA to tow her out and take her home, so she trimmed ours at Giles's farm a few days later, and he took them to Worcester for us.

Unfortunately, one of the ewes being a twit on the trimming stand, caught her chin on the headpiece and ended up with a large soft swelling under her jaw, which we thought would mean we couldn't take her. By sale day it had gone down sufficiently for her to go through the ring, although mention of the problem did put buyers off, understandably, and she returned home to fight another day. It was far too early to undervalue them.

The main highlight of the day was her companion who, although I felt looked the part, still surprised us by achieving top price for a Blue Texel at this sale. She travelled to a new home in the north of England that evening and hopefully will breed her purchaser some lovely lambs.

As we neared the end of the month, we were still praying for some substantial rain. In fairness, I was thoroughly enjoying the weather, as were the sheep and lambs. When the wind eased that was – because couldn't it blow! So cold it drained any moisture out of the ground, but hey-ho when it ceased for a little while, the sun was warm and we could almost kid ourselves summer was approaching. We actually lunched on the lawn with another sheep breeder friend and it was so hot, we moved the table into the shade of the bare branches of the laburnum tree.

But nature copes with all the stresses better than we humans. The copper beech that hangs over the Stroud road like a pink waterfall was a stunning colour at the moment. The fresh leaves only stay this incredible flesh colour for a few days before gradually darkening to their intense copper red. Although lacking anything green in the well-grazed fields, the verdant colour of the verges mingling with the startling yellow of oil seed rape just coming into flower really did encourage us to think of summer.

We had one field with fresh grass, just below North farm, where Aub's Texel gimmers were having the luxury of being turned out. The Blue gimmers, still feeling the cold in the fresh mornings, were on less good ground, but with sufficient hard food and hay were still growing on well, and seem fairly unconcerned. Obviously, they didn't know the whites had priority.

Such excitement. Rain overnight. Not a huge amount but enough to freshen up the grass and the trees a little. Mind you, I almost got excited at eight spots the previous evening. Shows how desperate we were getting. Aub moved the ewes with older lambs onto the Ruin field, as it appeared to be greener than their present one.

Then it was my turn to move some sheep. We still had a few 'iffy' ones that were coming in at nights and the fricking animals went everywhere when I turned them out. My fault for telling Aub to take the dogs, so I was doing it on my own, but he was struggling with the ones he moved onto the Ruin two days ago. They weren't sure it was where they wanted to be that morning.

Mine only had to cross the yard to the field they'd been in for the past week. Obviously fed up with no grass, several legged it towards Througham, as Aub had left all the gates open, while another headed to Miserden with her children. I might have sorted them, had a Blue ewe not forgotten her children and headed to the field alone, meaning I had to chase her lambs out to follow her. No point in trying to do anything without a dog, so I left them where they were, just relieved to discover the family that appeared to be heading for Miserden were enjoying the grass just inside the farm gate. I secured that, so they couldn't actually leave the area.

Then, after a restorative coffee, with Maisie's help we managed to return all the escapees to their rightful fields.

Maisie

Sidney and sister

MAY

I was starting to feel a light could be seen at the end of the bottle feeding tunnel. Well, at least I was on my last bag of milk powder and refusing to buy more. Mind you, it was a 20kg bag, so should last the remaining lambs on bottles until the end of the month, and I decided I might not need that if the latest ones to be taken off the bucket feeder got their act together. Jill was helping with bottle feeds as she always enjoyed doing, although her favourite occupation in the milk shed was finding Rich Tea biscuits.

I'd just moved the last three lambs from the ad-lib warm milk machine to milk bottles on a rack, as at five weeks they tend to gorge themselves and die if the milk isn't limited. Ideally, I keep them on milk for eight weeks, as weaning them at five, as some do, seems a little harsh. The change from machine back to bottles is usually fairly uneventful, but these three thought I was flourishing a machine gun at them, rather than offering them bottles, so I took them off the rack and fed each individually. This eventually worked, although they refused to take much milk, so on to plan B. They didn't get lunch! Hopefully they'd be hungry by teatime and more amenable to my offer.

By day four, two of them sucked the bottles on the rack, one going straight in, having grasped that it was safe the previous evening. The second eyed the rack with caution, but seeing his friend was sucking, decided to join in; however the third still felt he was in a danger zone, and a bottle might turn into a hand grenade at any point. Once I climbed into the pen and secured him on the teat, he sucked for England. I hoped they'd still be engaging brain at teatime.

Then there is Silly Sidney (named by a grandchild). His sister had always been twice his size, and took priority over both sides of their mother's udder, leaving just the dregs for poor Sidney. Eventually I decided he'd have to join the bottle lambs and left his mother with her enormous daughter as a single.

Sidney, of course, wouldn't suck a bottle. I'd tried him while still with his mother to no avail, and just hoped once he was really hungry, he'd see sense. Not our Sidney. I moved him in with four others who were on bottles, and hoped they might instil some sense into him, but no, Sidney stood his ground. He was not opening his mouth.

Well he did when I tubed him, (pouring milk

directly into his stomach through a plastic tube), as he was going to die otherwise. Sidney's contribution to tubing was to chew the pipe as determinedly as he could, puncturing the plastic in several places. After two or three sessions I was back to trying to convince him that sucking a bottle of warm milk wasn't quite the hardship he was making it out to be. Then, eventually, one day, he sucked. Not a terribly orthodox method, more suck, pull, gurgle, choke, repeat, but he did take some milk down before the gurgle, choke action. However, if this was how he'd treated his mother's udder, I could appreciate why she elected to stop feeding him. The sucking did get better, although it took a painfully long time to get a quarter of a pint of milk into him, but he was still alive.

For those who remember the old-fashioned tents, rectangular in shape, with a main pole running down the centre, and sides that fell in if the guy ropes weren't tight enough, well that's what Sidney looked like. His backbone standing out and very little flesh over his ribs. Not a pretty sight. By now I'd decided that Sidney was looking so sad, his cuddle and bottle were as much for his mental health as nutrition. After I'd fed the other four in the stable, who all happily drank their half pint from the rack at speed, I would sit on a bale of straw, and endeavour to get about a third of a pint down his throat before we both lost the will to live.

Thankfully Sidney eventually started to eat sufficient creep pellets, as his sucking never really improved.

He still got cuddles, and his intake of feed eventually tightened his guy ropes considerably. Soon they would all join the other weaned lambs, out in a grass paddock during the day, but still with ad lib feed and a warm bed at nights. By the time the main flock were weaned, hopefully these would have caught up with them. I'd certainly help them try.

Life at Bisley Lane Farm was all about pigs again. Another trip to market for some more weaners, as Mark felt he was running short. His homebreds and the first weaners he purchased some time ago had all become pork and sausages, after they'd grown on in the woods, apart from the Supercars; Bugatti, Porche and Ferrari.

The Supercars were all Pietrain x Gloucester Old Spots and they would hopefully farrow in a few weeks' time after Chorizo, who had been reprieved from sausages, was now being kept as a boar.

The youngest pork pigs in the wood – the Berkshires Mark had bought two months ago – were dwindling in numbers, having been eaten, so more were needed to grow on happily in this idyllic outdoor space. Unfortunately, the world and his friend were desperate for pigs, so on Thursday we came home with an empty trailer.

As it happened, this was probably the best result as Bugatti gave birth to ten piglets on Saturday afternoon, a good three weeks earlier than anticipated. The reason why Chorizo hadn't seemed too interested in the

Supercars when put in with them three months ago may be that one of their brothers got there first before they were separated, and they were already in pig!

By sheer luck Tom, who works for Mark, wanted to bring his little boy up to see the pigs, as Mark usually only feeds them in the mornings. When they arrived they discovered the new family. Soon our entire family, who had been visiting us, were all assisting with the rehousing, as it did look as though Porsche wasn't going to be far behind her sister, and at this moment in time all three gilts and Chorizo were wallowing in mud in the wood, with Bugatti having staked her claim on the one pig ark they'd all been sharing.

Aub and Kevin went to collect the trailer, because that also meant unloading the repaired steam cleaner we'd picked up the previous evening and it was a two-man job to unload. I'd moved a further group of bottle lambs from one of the stables to join the older ones in the sheep shed, thus leaving two stables available for pigs. While I continued preparing the stables and feeding the remaining bottle lambs, Aub and Kev went back to Bisley Lane to collect the pigs.

Porsche would go in one stable, while Ferrari and Chorizo would reside in the black fronted shed for a while, as they needed moving from the pen in the woods before Bugatti and her family could be evacuated. I gathered this was causing some concern as it was raining again and Chorizo and the other two gilts had decided they'd also like to be inside in the dry.

Luckily Aub had found a piece of corrugated tin that he was able to fix across the front of the ark, and Toby was standing in the doorway making sure there were no invaders.

Fairly soon the two gilts and Chorizo arrived at our farm, Chorizo and Ferrari manoeuvred into the black shed and Porsche established in her new stable. She certainly did look as though farrowing could be fairly imminent. Aub and Kevin then returned to the woods to collect the new family. This apparently went without too many hitches, although wading round in deep mud did slow things down a bit. They had a gate in the trailer so the piglets could be put in the front section, and holding the final piglet in front of Bugatti, Kev persuaded her she ought to join in and she eventually wandered into the trailer.

Soon she was established in her new home, deep in straw in the second stable, with a separate area with shavings on the floor and a heat lamp over the top, where the piglets could escape from their mother, allowing her a bit of peace and quiet as well. After the chaos of mud with children running around in excitement, in the way these things happen, all suddenly became calm. The livestock all appeared to be happy and by now we'd worn out the grandchildren too. With a car full of filthy and exhausted kids, Kate took them home. Rather her than me.

Well, the swallows have arrived. I thought I'd seen

some circling a few days ago, but I was quite sure when one crash landed in the yard in front of me. It even surprised the dogs, who stood completely still, watching it, but it very quickly gathered itself up and flew over the roof. Never seen one do that before, but it had been a long flight!

A couple of days later, Porsche was definitely showing all the signs of nesting in the adjacent stable, and started to give birth about 7.30 in the evening. The first two piglets were produced with great ease, but then nothing for a couple of hours. Porsche appeared to be very uncomfortable, pushing and straining, so Mark investigated. Finding a piglet that was stuck, he was able to push it back from the birth canal, but then felt perhaps we should contact a vet, so I was told to ring the duty vet that evening.

Luckily it was Paul, who had helped out when Spot had her tragic farrowing, but he emphasised there was little that could be done, other than giving Oxytocin, which would hopefully open her up and encourage her to push. Mark might have solved the problem by pushing the awkward piglet back. I passed the information on to Aub and Mark at the farm.

"She's just pushed out another one," Aub said. "Oh, and another. I'll inject her anyway as it should help, but hopefully everything will be OK now."

"Paul did suggest leaving her quietly on her own," I tentatively mentioned, but knew Mark would be staying with her until she had given birth to every one of them.

Eventually she finished, with nine live piglets, the final one ejected dead, but probably this was the one that had been stuck and squashed earlier on. So sad to have lost one, but Porsche seemed happy with her family and was eventually left in peace for the night.

The following morning it was lovely to look over both stable doors and see both sows lying happily stretched out feeding their families. Bugatti's were already growing on well. But more pig dramas were in store for the next day.

Having an appointment to see the consultant at 9.45am, I decided to feed the bottle lambs and the seven dodgy ewes with lambs still in at nights, before breakfast. The sound of water running and a powerful smell of pigs greeted me as I arrived at the yard. I knew immediately what had happened. Chorizo and Ferrari had got bored, so for amusement had turned the water trough upside down. In doing so they had made their home into a swamp, something they probably enjoyed, but the pig effluent now flooding down the yard was not pleasant.

After conferring on the phone with Aub, who couldn't remember what I was doing, he suggested I went in and picked the trough up. Looking over the door, acknowledging the flood was deep enough for wellies, which I was not wearing, and the fact that Chorizo was attempting to leave, I declined this offer. Not sure I'd be appreciated at the hospital smelling of pigs, and it's a perfume difficult to remove even in a shower. No, this was one excitement I could happily leave Mark and Aubrey to sort out.

The two pig families were thankfully happy in their stables, which were properly set up for them. The black shed was not ideal for pigs, but had been the only place we could put the other two on Saturday, as it has a concrete floor and a safe gate they couldn't remove. Returning home, unscathed, just as Aub was leaving, I suggested he took his wellies with him as he was likely to be involved with the pig department, and it was quite deep.

My hospital appointment was to see the consultant about my knee replacement, and as I'd struggled wearing jeans on my last appointment, I looked through my wardrobe for a skirt. There was one hanging up but it would take a fair amount of imagination on my part for me to get into it and do the top button up. I decided if I had to use the second or third button down as a waist band, it buttoned all down the front, I would look as though I was back in the mini skirt era, and although the legs weren't bad in the sixties, I thought I'd pass on that today. Eventually I found the skirt I'd really been looking for, typically screwed up in the back of a draw, but looking a far better fit.

I couldn't remember when I'd last ironed something, but the iron and board were still in residence in Heather's old bedroom, and ironing must be a bit like riding a bike, because it all came back to me immediately. The skirt was made of a number of panels, all of which I ironed to perfection, and to my utter surprise when I tried it on it actually fitted. I could even do the top button up. Searching around for a top, I selected a navy and white striped one Heather had given me for a present, then matched this with navy and white summer shoes. All a bit chilly, but it wasn't actually raining at this point. Topped off with my dark red wax jacket I thought it would pass muster.

Typically, today the consultant didn't even glance at my knee, other than to point out the operation was the most complex, as I'm knock kneed when most people are bow legged. Always like a doctor with a good bedside manner! Luckily his secretary was most amenable. We sorted out a date for the operation just after the only show we appeared to be going to this year, at the beginning of July.

Chorizo and Rari were now resident in the grain store, until they wrecked that trough as well! We're not really set up to be a pig farm.

The rain kept on coming. Feeling sorry for the seven dodgy ewes and lambs in the two acre, I went up earlier than usual to let them back in to their dry barn for the night. Watching from the gate, having shouted to them to hurry up, I thought the slowest was making more progress than she was and foolishly moved the piece of wood that usually kept the heavy metal gate firmly shut. The old Texel who always wants to come in first, pushed her head through the gate and kept on pushing. I couldn't hold it shut. Then somehow, as she pushed, she trapped my foot under the bottom rung, knocking me over, and still pushing. Thankfully I shouted at her loudly enough and smacked her on the head, hoping she'd back off and see she had plenty of room to come in through the opening gateway, once she extricated her head from the gate.

It's horrific when you can see a serious accident waiting to happen, as I knew if she carried on pushing, head down, she would then stand upright and take the gate off its hinges, and I was still pinned under the bottom rung, squelching in the mud and cursing. Luckily for me she saw sense and headed for the shed, galloping along to overtake those that had gone past her. Even the slow one was heading in before I managed to get my foot out from under the gate. Had the worst happened I could have been seriously injured, I know. Next time they can stay out in the rain.

Later that evening Aub and Mark selected the next two pigs to become sausages. This happened more easily than anticipated, as the older pigs were still ploughing around in the muddy woods. They would go to the abattoir the next day, but were secured for the night in the now less flooded black shed, with a dry bed at one end. Not ideal but we really were running out of secure pig premises.

The next day wasn't out best. One of Porsche's

piglets was found dead. She may have laid on it, we just don't know. It was the smallest so perhaps wasn't getting enough milk. Whatever the reason it's always so sad.

So was the fact that Jilly no longer had much quality of life. The previous evening I'd found her marching round her run and tried to put her to bed twice, but certainly the first time she got up again and continued walking. Along with some sort of dementia her arthritis must be painful, although she is dosed daily with Loxicom, and her eyesight was no longer good. Difficult to tell with her hearing as that could often be selective, but the circling was the major problem.

It was a warm, sunny morning, far nicer than the previous few days and Jilly elected to ride to the farm in my car, which now looks and smells like a damp kennel. Not all Jilly's fault as Jess seems incapable of grasping that dogs sit in the back, and arrives in the passenger seat as soon as I get in, so my black leather seats are covered in mud. At first Jilly opted to stay in the back when I opened the rear door, her chin resting on the back seat, so I left her there while I collected the feed for the few ewes in the shed. When I next passed the car it was empty, so she'd either got out or fallen out, not sure which, but soon I saw her striding round the farmyard. At least at the farm she felt at home and her circling was in big loops round the different yards and buildings, following me when possible. After doing the lambs bottles, I knew I must ring our vets. Flick answered and when I explained the situation arranged for Tamsin to be with us about 10.30.

I was still sorting the bottle lambs when Aub drove into the yard to collect the trailer. One of his best Texel gimmers was in the field with a broken leg. No idea how she'd done it, but it looked like complex fracture around the fetlock joint of a back leg, so she must have caught it in the hayrack or fence. I helped him catch her and we brought her back to the yard, making a small pen for her in the new shed.

I spoke to Flick again, and added a broken leg to the morning's visit, although I was hopeful the gimmer had dislocated it at that point. Once we'd settled the ewe in the pen Aub continued his feeding and checking, being gone for ages, which gave me a good ten minutes of talking to and cuddling Jill after I'd put her in the back of the car. I then decided to take her home with me while I collected milk for coffee at the farm, and put some washing on the line. Having sent Aub a text explaining my movements, I was later enlightened that he and the dogs were pursuing ewes and lambs through the woods, where some walker had left the gate open.

Unloading Jilly at home, I directed her towards the house rather than the kennel, as she always liked to help with domestic chores, and she wandered round the garden while I put the washing out. Then equipped with milk we journeyed back to the farm. I lifted Jilly out of the car again, and put the kettle on for coffee while Jill wandered around, then sat outside the milk shed in the sunshine and called her to me. I drank coffee while she consumed rich tea biscuits, something she was always fond of doing. Bending down to eat a crumb she'd dropped, she laid down beside me in the sun where I chatted to her, stroking her head and ears and feeding her more biscuits.

Tammy and Aub arrived at the same time, Aub having fed at North Farm and taken the other dogs home. It was the right time. Without any fuss, Jilly just lying in the sunshine, enjoying the warmth and having a final cuddle and biscuit, we said Goodbye to one of our most wonderful sheepdogs. Later Aub buried her out on the hill overlooking Verandas alongside Nell and Kim. Three of our best working dogs, still keeping an eye on the sheep.

That night I cried for her. She'd had a wonderful life, but somewhere between 'hello' and 'goodbye' there was so much love and so many memories.

Jilly

Toby with Ferrari's piglets

MID MAY

Tamsin worked miracles on the gimmer with the break, which she confirmed was a complex injury. At first she was doubtful she could do anything for the injury, but I quietly explained that Aub had lost one of his best ewes on her back the day before, and with our loss of Jilly, she was going to have to try. Bandaged with a splint rather than plastered, as the injury was on the actual joint, we kept our fingers crossed for a full recovery.

The next day, the gimmer was looking good. The bandage looked secure and her leg was straight. She could stand on it, so fingers crossed.

I took my car to Tesco to see if the newly returned car wash team could restore it. They'd been shut all through lockdown and it was rather obvious that the poor car had been used as my dog carrier all winter. It probably wouldn't have looked so bad if Jess could have contained herself and stayed in the back like she was supposed to, but if her owner lets her sit in the front of the gator while he drives, it isn't surprising if she thinks she should be able to do the same in my car. Considering just how wet and muddy it's been for the past few months it doesn't take much imagination to envisage the state of my Subaru.

The man I spoke to was appalled when he saw it. Yes, they could do it but it would take two hours and cost me £85. I was horrified. I did realise I was asking a lot, but £85 was more than I expected it to cost. He called his boss over who asked me what I thought I'd have to pay and we negotiated at £55.

Dragging my shopping time out to last an hour can be a struggle, but trying to make it take two hours was beyond me. Luckily the café was open and I managed to make a cup of tea and a panini last for over an hour before I could collect my transport.

Glancing through the windows I had to admit my car looked fantastic, but the cleaner then insisted on giving me a guided tour of all he'd done, so proud of the result and I couldn't blame him. I agreed it looked wonderful and was well worth the money and thanked him very much. Now it was just a case of finding the right switches to turn all the lights and controls off that he appeared to have washed too enthusiastically, but we'd sort it.

Yet another sheep on its back. They were so heavy

in wool and in any normal year would be sheared by now. This time the unfortunate animal was a Charolais x Texel ram. We brought him in and treated him with antibiotics, but he'd been on his back too long and didn't survive, his lungs full of fluids.

We were now on pig patrol. Mark, Kate and the children had all headed for our cottage in Wales, leaving us in charge. Come Sunday evening we were then leaving Mark T looking after everything because we were heading off to a sale. It felt a bit odd just passing everything over to him. He didn't have to worry about the dogs because they'd gone to kennels for Sunday night, but he was a little concerned should Ferrari farrow on his watch.

"Just let her get on with it, or if a major drama, call the vet," was really the only answer I could give. This was a planned pregnancy after all, with Chorizo as father, and our son was confident he could go off on holiday! We were only set to be away for about 36 hours, so hopefully we should be back before she produced anything.

Aub put fly repellent on most of the ewes and lambs, as the weather was meant to come really warm and the ewes wouldn't be sheared for at least another week. The plan had been for the remaining gimmers and the shearling rams to be sheared on Thursday. By 7pm Aub was fed up with sheep, so the Blues had to wait until the following Tuesday to be done when we returned.

What a beautiful morning for a journey. Birds everywhere shouting about the weather and warning others off their territory. We were hoping to head for Skipton fairly early, but with pigs and cows to do as well as sheep, and showing Mark T where everything was, this all took time. The weaners were still living in the very muddy woods, thoroughly enjoying life. It was certainly a lovely place to be, now it had stopped raining and the warm sunlight was penetrating through the trees. Aub said he laughed when Mark T struggled to feed them on Sunday, when being shown where they were. Tuesday morning I laughed when Aub couldn't pull his feet out of the mud. We fly treated several older, dirty ewes in the two acre before we left, and eventually headed off around midday, hoping the roads would be quiet.

You had to be joking! Easing out of lockdown obviously meant everyone was on the M5 and M6 over the Bank holiday. Actually, that couldn't be true because both Mark in Wales, and Heather on holiday in Devon, said the beaches were teeming with people, but we still couldn't believe just how much traffic there was on the M5 on a Sunday afternoon. Shouldn't they have got where they're going by now? We also noticed how gleamingly clean nearly every car was. Do normal people all polish their cars on Sunday mornings before clogging up the motorway, or had they just polished them to death during lockdown? They had to have done it that day because my car, which had been cleaned four days ago was now sadly dribbled with dust and rain marks.

It was at this point I asked myself why we were going all the way to Skipton, with only one sheep to sell? Again, it was Giles's fault. He talked us into it, as he talked us into taking the gimmer to Worcester. Not a bad move, but driving all the way to Skipton, on a Bank holiday, did make me wonder. Traffic was always moving, but slowed to almost a standstill as we merged with the M6. Around Stafford we stopped at the services, when we eventually found somewhere to park. It was manic, so we purchased a sandwich and coffee as quickly as possible and headed back to the car. I think I fell asleep after this, as things did appear to have cleared when I was next aware of anything, although Aub was muttering about signs warning of delays around Preston. Scrabbling in the back I located the map and suggested we took the M65 before we reached Preston, but this was disregarded. When Aub drove North, to see relations etc. he always came off at Preston. As it happened the satnav also suggested we took the M65, so grudgingly he agreed, and gradually motorway gave way to country roads and wonderful scenery.

Giles, who was bringing our lone gimmer up with five of his, met us at the market, where one of the market staff let us in and showed us where to unload. Most people wouldn't be there until Monday.

Giles and family were booked at the Travel Lodge,

but somehow I'd made a boob with our booking, so we were staying at a local pub, where we all had a great meal that night. Our room was small, but adequate, but the sound of an industrial fridge going all night wasn't great, although I think I slept quite well. Aub said he didn't, but I don't always believe him.

Not much action at the market at eight when we arrived, but people soon turned up. There weren't many Blue Texels, but it was also a commercial sheep sale, and there were a great number of ewes with quite young lambs that went through the ring after the Blues. It was a lovely market, where we felt welcomed and an auctioneer who knew how to sell pedigree animals. Both our gimmer and Giles' sold well. After a fraught half hour taking the sheep out to a patch of grass to be photographed, most of them having been barely handled before, we all headed south again just after midday.

This time the satnav agreed with Aub and took us back to Preston. Lovely along the country lanes, but major traffic jam as we approached the M6, although it gradually cleared and we were on our way home. Traffic again, unbelievable, but glad we weren't going north as all four lanes were stationary on that side for about the next ten or twelve miles. Even when it cleared, it was slow. It was obviously good timing to have left when we did, as a traffic report as we neared home spoke of holdups behind us due to a major accident, but we kept moving, although mainly at 50 miles an hour.

Just after we reached the M5, the pig owner rang from one of the Welsh beaches, with a pig alert. He was viewing the camera in the stables on his phone and Ferrari was licking a piglet. Better that than eating one, we assured him. He was delighted to know we were only an hour away from home, which was slightly optimistic, and would check as soon as we got there. Never a dull moment with all the farming enterprises. When we arrived Ferrari had eight babies, and she then produced two more, so was happily a mother of ten. The last was a little bit smaller, but Aub picked it up out of the straw and plugged it onto a teat and it didn't look back.

Sitting in the sun on the patio, drinking a cup of tea a little later, we rang to report back to the pig farmer, only to be asked if we'd sprayed their navels? Having to admit that we'd failed to do this so far, we assured him we would immediately adjourn to the yard again to do so. That was a drama in itself, because when one of the piglets screamed as Aub picked it up, Ferrari swung round with great force, mouth open and teeth like a crocodile, nearly knocking Aub over. Eventually peace reigned again, babies were fished out of deep straw where Ferrari had flung them, or trodden on them, as she hadn't really learnt to be the most caring of mothers at that point, but the following morning all seemed fine.

Pigs in the lambing pens

JUNE

The lambs were growing on, some really standing out as possible show stock. It's funny but when you have a field full of good lambs it's far more difficult to select the best than when only a couple have caught your eye. Usually there is a star in every field; one that has stood out for several weeks. Often Aub will say he has a show lamb in the eighteen acre and I'll know immediately which one.

They were still with their mothers at the moment – it was only June – although the lambs had access to creep feed in a covered trough, too tight for their mothers to fit alongside. These really good lambs were either ones with the best growth rate or simply strong enough to be the first in the creep each day and eaten more. There is nothing scientific about judging this!

The bottle lambs were also looking well, with Sidney

well-fleshed and thriving.

With the pandemic still prevalent and lockdown tying us all at home, we realised quite early on that our local Royal Three Counties Show would not be on again this year. A great disappointment, but wonderful to see the Devon County Show was still aiming to happen, albeit in a much smaller way than usual. Later in the year than normal, this was to run for three days at the beginning of July, with different breeds on different days. Again, it was Giles who prompted us to enter, assuring us that it would be great fun to have a small, but select party. The Texels and Blue Texels were being shown at the same time on the Friday, so we opted to just enter Blues.

Our lockdown puppy Jess was now living in the kennels with Maisie. Jess finally blotted her copybook by eating two of the three beautiful pink geraniums I'd bought. Forgetting her vandalism, I placed their pots just outside the front door. Only when she came in from having a wee did I discover two pots empty, the contents all over the porch floor, but unrecognisable as any sort of plant. Amazingly she missed one, which went on to bloom magnificently.

Aub says I'm being totally unfair, but in all honesty the sheepdogs are far happier in their own department, it's warm at night and an ideal time for her to go out. She's had over a month of staying in the kennel during the day, after we'd been round the sheep in the mornings, so it was nothing new to her. I think Maisie was pleased to have her friend back.

Blue Texels have been in the UK for the past twenty years, but recently they've been followed by both the Dassenkop (Badgerface Texels) and the Dutch Spotted Sheep. The Spotteds have never really appealed to me, though they are very popular and very expensive. I judged some in an Any Other Breed class at a west country show a couple of years ago. I asked the owner whether they were a meat or milk breed (never having come across them before) and became even more confused when she didn't know the answer. They didn't appear to have great carcases, but I have seen better since.

They just don't do it for me, but the Badgerface Texels are smart. I've always admired the Torwen Badger Face Welsh Mountain for their colouring and these are the same. A dark body, almost black, with creamy coloured eyebrows, chin, belly and legs. Badgerface Texels not only look really smart, but have a fantastic carcase.

Having discussed the breed over coffee a few times, we decided to buy a ram lamb to put on some of our Blue ewes and see what colour they came out. Apparently the first Badgerface Texels came from Blue stock, which is permissible with the breed Society, so I contacted our friend Janet in Northern Ireland who keeps this breed. She was selling some in an online sale at the beginning of June, so I looked up the entries.

While we hadn't really contemplated buying a ewe, I fancied one she had for sale, Apricot, with her two lambs, Chilli and Cherry. Aub was smitten with a gimmer of Janet's. She was certainly a stunner, but I've praised Janet many times for her excellent trimmer and photographer! She laughed, but did say she was a good sheep. I thought she might be far too expensive, but Aub was not to be dissuaded and we bid for both. The auction was held online over three days. The final day was also the day our shearling rams were being sheared at Edgeworth, which was causing a few problems. My job was to sit and watch the auction finish, which after a while actually became a little like watching paint dry.

The online sale had entries from many different breeds, but it was just the Badgerface and Blue Texels I was really following. During the latter part of the morning prices for some sheep were changing, while others hadn't yet acquired a bid. I put a large enough bid on Apricot to feel quite hopeful about securing her. I was already winning her and well under my maximum. I also had the gimmer for the moment, although expected her to go much further. We hoped to acquire four doses of semen from the gimmer's sire, she and Apricot were out of the same ewe, but not identical breeding. If we won all lots we would secure a breeding programme!

Eventually boredom set in and I wandered off to the kitchen to ponder about lunch, and was still wondering what culinary delight to produce for Aub when he got back, when an email came through saying we'd won the gimmer and the semen. I glanced at the clock. Surely I hadn't been that long. The sale finished at twelve and it had only been eleven when I wandered off. I was worried then as Apricot was five lots prior to the gimmer, so rushed back to the office. My laptop was still showing her page and my lower bid. I flicked back through the sale entries, some had sold, but others were still up, including Apricot.

At that point Janet messaged me from Ireland to say the site had crashed. Nothing indicating this at my end, but I shut everything down, waited impatiently for a minute then opened up the sale again. It still showed me winning Apricot, but I couldn't reach any of the other pages. Eleven fifty now. I rang the auctioneers, who apologised and assured me they were getting it back up as soon as possible. Then Mark T rang me to say one of the tups they'd started shearing was panting and looking distraught.

"Leave it well alone," I think I shouted down the phone. "I can't come down at the moment. I'll try to find Aub. Don't try to finish shearing it."

Aub had just returned from collecting barley. I told him he'd have to deal with the shearers as I was still trying to sort out the sale. The site eventually came back up, but only just before the ewe was due to finish. She was still my bid, although £500 more than five minutes ago, but I think it had just stuck on her previous price. Thank goodness I'd put on a higher maximum bid. As her Lot number went green and said I'd won her, a message pinged to say I'd been outbid on the gimmer. I raised mine by £400 but was still outbid and didn't have time to raise it again before she was sold.

All things considered I was lucky having not only bought the ewe with her lambs, but also the semen we wanted, so we could use this on Apricot. I phoned the auctioneers to tell them what I thought about their sale, to which they were, again, apologetic. I suppose the learning curve is to make sure my top bid is on any lot I definitely want right from the beginning.

Travel arrangements would be made for the sheep to at least reach Carlisle, but as it happened, they were to be delivered to Shrewsbury, which was a great relief. Another relief was that the shearling ram, half sheared on auction day, was now parted from his wool and looking perfectly happy out with the others. He'd simply overheated, poor thing, waiting to be shorn.

After a warm day, one of the greatest pleasures is witnessing the evening ritual of lambs doing wacky races in the front field. They gather in a group under the stone wall, then one suddenly dashes off across the field. Seconds later the others stream after him, leaping in the air with happiness and exhilaration as they go. Then suddenly they all turn and race back along the bottom of the field, past their grazing, unconcerned mothers, curving round to gallop back to the top again. They remind me of a starling murmuration, all coordinating together. Total time wasters and we could watch them for hours. When they tire, they wander around in groups, jumping over bits of wood the winter has abandoned in their field, leaping up on all fours like circus animals. Suddenly a raucous baa emits from one of the ewes and her lambs charge towards her, ducking their heads and thumping her udder to encourage her to let down milk for their next meal, lifting her backend off the ground. There is no subtlety with their technique.

My birthday coincided with the day the last of the ewes lambed, a sweet little ram lamb appearing in the front field. The swallows that nest in the eaves of the shed had accepted the pigs, and some were nesting in Ferrari's stable. We kept seeing the parents flying in with beaks full of straw to line their mud nest.

Suddenly, I had nothing too pressing to do, except a lovely family barbeque with wine and presents at Mark and Kates' with Heather and Kevin and all the grandchildren in the evening. Not having taken my phone, we arrived home to a text from our neighbour Tim – a ewe looked unwell, outside their kitchen window. With Tim's help, Aub got her in and treated her, although not sure of the problem. I'd drunk too much to be useful, so went to bed.

Clemmie was living in the sheep shed in the daytime now that we were a major pig farm and all the stables were occupied. I didn't think she minded

– she can probably see more from there than being shut in the yard. A new friend Dougal came to live with us, and was also resident in the sheep shed in the daytime. A very handsome 'silver unicorn' belonging to our neighbour Sam. Sadly, his previous companion developed laminitis, and the combination of age and ailment forced the decision to have her put down, but Dougal has settled in well with us. There can be a bit of squealing and the odd shrill whinny of complaint if Clemmie is taken out for ride, leaving him on his own, but generally they ignore each other in a friendly sort of way. When turned out together at night eating is the most important thing on the agenda.

Tamsin changed the bandage on the ewe with a broken leg. This would come off in two weeks if all was well. The joint was quite straight and seemed to be improving – incredible really, but such a relief. She checked the sick ewe Aub and Tim had brought in and prescribed antibiotics.

When I called the bottle lambs in that evening, a distant plaintive bleat told me Sidney had somehow got into the 12 acre with his head stuck in the fence looking back at the shed. No idea how he'd got there, as he'd have to have limbo danced under the gate, but only Sidney could do this. Extricating his head was fairly easy and he trotted along behind me to the gateway then galloped across the paddock to the shed, concerned that supper may have all gone before he got there. They were practically on ad-lib pellets so he needn't have worried.

Yesterday Aub said he'd got the lambs in early as it was so hot outside. When I reached the yard, three were wandering around. Pity he doesn't ever remember to count them in. I expect these had been sleeping under the trailer in the shade.

A text arrived at about eleven-thirty in the evening to confirm our new Badgerface sheep coming from Northern Ireland would arrive at Shrewsbury around 1pm the next day. So today, after feeding we set off to collect them. The sick ewe Aub had brought in still looked off colour, but hopefully the antibiotics and painkillers would keep her going. We'd checked her for maggots and this wasn't her problem. As usual things didn't go quite to plan and we were a bit late leaving, the satnav saying we'd be at our destination a 1.10pm.

As is often the case, Aub couldn't make up his mind which way to go, but considering the speed he drove through Whiteway, cursing every vehicle we met, I suggested we'd be better off on the motorway. We left the M5 just after Worcester and headed for Kidderminster, which proved an easy route up to Shrewsbury.

When we arrived at the farm, our sheep were in a pen being refreshed with hay and water along with the one we hadn't managed to buy, but we were delighted with our purchases. A number of others were in an adjacent pen and it was interesting to see them in real life, having just seen their pictures on the website.

Apricot and her children were lovely, and we were pleased with a Blue ram lamb we'd bought privately from Janet. They travelled home well in our trailer, arriving about half past three when we settled them in isolation pens for a few days, although near to others not to feel alone. This would finish in two weeks if all was well.

Mark T and Jeremy would be shearing the ewes on Saturday, so I suggested we got them in on Friday night. The weather was dry but the dew so heavy the ewes had been wet in the mornings. Aub muttered for so long about the difficulty of bringing them in overnight, separating lambs off and lack of facilities with pigs residing in most buildings. By the time he'd finished making excuses I'd forgotten what my suggestion had been. Anyway, the decision was no, but on Saturday morning the ewes were wet. Luckily, I appeared to be the only person concerned about this, so no problem.

That evening we watched Jeremy Clarkson's new programme about his farm. I've never been very keen on the man, on Top Gear he was partying around with cars, doing just what he wanted and getting paid an outrageous amount. That fact was obviously true if he could purchase a 1000 acre farm in the North Cotswolds, but it was the funniest programme I'd seen for years. I even felt slightly sorry for his predicament and lack of knowledge.

In recent months the 'escape to farming' and

countryside type programmes have been so overdone in my opinion, with presenters acting more like Laurel and Hardy than farmers, or turning into domestic goddesses in between lambing sheep, they made me cringe. Clarkson exposed the genuine problems most farmers encounter on a daily basis, with a realism that brought a breath of fresh air.

Shearing took place on a day of blazing heat, confusion and far too much work. Starting just after six, Aub brought the first field of ewes in with the dubious help of both dogs and a foul temper. As they ran past me into the handling unit he shouted, "Jabbed that lamb once already. I'll have to do him again."

130 sheep had just come past me at speed, I had no idea which he was talking about.

"The one with an ear down."

That obviously would have clarified the situation if I'd noticed it pass by, but I hadn't. I gathered he was indicating he'd already treated the lamb with antibiotics, but it looked as though it needed some more. Aub started shouting a lot of other instructions and responses to my questions, with lambs bleating loudly, having been separated from their mothers. I do wish he would just say Yes or No then I might understand what he means.

With pigs in all our useful buildings, we decided to run the lambs back to Betty's field, where their mothers could re-join them once sheared, but I almost lost one group as they tried to run back while I was struggling to close the gate. We were still waiting for Dave to fix the gatepost – based on past experience this could be a long wait.

Once we'd collected the second lot from the Quarry field and run the Blues up from the bottom fields it was almost ten o'clock. I had two lamb carcases to pick up from the butchers for Edgeworth Polo Club's barbeque before joining my Zoom meeting with fellow writers scheduled for eleven. I changed at speed and drove to Nailsworth, where Saturday morning traffic was a nightmare. All collected and delivered by 11.15, so joined the group, dodging backwards and forwards to put chicken in the oven and scrape new potatoes as Giles and Sally were coming to lunch and to see the new sheep, something that had been arranged before we knew the shearers were coming today.

Gradually the day fell into place, with a leisurely lunch, and I gave them a tour of Blues and the new Badgerface Texels, while Aub moved the final ewes up to the yard for Mark and Jeremy. Feeling guilty about the chaos earlier, I plied the shearers with ice creams before we went back for a cup of tea in the cool of the house. At least most of the sheep had sheared well, the temperature helping, though the men appeared a little worn. The ewes must have been relieved to lose their fleeces and looked fit and tidy.

Finally, quarantine ended for Apricot and family,

and they were now turned out in the Two Acre with my iffy sheep so I could keep an eye on them. Fabian, the Blue ram lamb with a posh name, was turned out with my bottle lambs as there was nowhere else to put him, but he seemed quite happy. Dougal's owner Sam admired him when she came to turn the ponies out and fell about laughing at his name.

"Definite Cheltenham College set then?"

"I thought he was named after one of my pop star heroes, in the sixties!"

Apricot and children
(reproduced with permission of Alfie Shaw)

MID JUNE

Clemmie and Dougal were getting on well. Sam and I have arranged that I'll get them both in in the mornings and she'll let them out late in the evening, when it's cooler. It makes such a pleasant change to have a welcoming whinny when I call Dougal in the mornings, and he trots up to me, happy to be coming inside in the shade. Not Clemmie. She doesn't move towards me at all. If I take Dougal into the sheep shed, where he's separated by a piece of electric fence tape, she either bolts for the gate and I catch her, or she takes off in the opposite direction until I get close enough to stand on the lunge rein attached to her head collar. She is a pony I will never work out, but she loves it when the children play with her and ride her.

I slept through the alarm, but was surprised to come downstairs to the front door wide open and no sign of Aub anywhere. I then remembered he and son Mark were heading to the abattoir with the second heifer today, which meant an early morning run. This still didn't explain his lack of security, leaving me in bed and the front door wide open!

My phone pinged, someone on the Miserden WhatsApp sent a reminder that the road was closed at the Fostons Ash. I had no idea of the whereabouts of the initial announcement of this closure, but rang Aub with the news. We are not isolated or even remote here really, although nine miles from any substantial town, but when the local council decide to dig up the road near the Foston's Ash it closes our main route to Gloucester and Cheltenham. Detours take us miles out of our way. With a truck and trailer, cow on board, it took the men over two hours to do the round trip to Whaddon which should have been forty minutes. The cow should have gone last week, but Kate forgot to book her in. With today's traffic chaos that's something she probably won't be allowed to forget for a while.

About an hour later I realised I'd have to work out a different route to Brockworth for a 'click and collect' order. I drove miles out of my way, making reversing an art form I don't usually master, as others I met seemed unable to back up. The last time this happened we had a buyer coming to collect two Blue gimmers and, as with this situation, would have changed our dates had we been made aware of the closure. If you reached the road-works site, there was probably one man down a hole and twenty-seven looking on.

These mid-June mornings are cooler, fresh. The birdsong sounds delicate and light, not raucous as it has been some mornings. Mind you, it doesn't take long to warm up, but the sheep have been checked and lambs fed by then. Pigville looking happy and contented. Aub mucked out, and power-washed the black shed, after Chorizo had made it into a quagmire.

Today the black shed had a new job – Aub, Mark and Toby, after bedding up one end with clean straw, moved Porsche and Bugatti and their families in there together. Toby marked Porsche and her piglets with purple spray so we could identify both families if a riot evolved. Luckily, after a bit of ear nipping, everyone settled down well. The piglets really enjoyed the space and galloped round like pink spotted balloons, bouncing off each other, stopping to argue then charging off again. I could stand and watch them for hours. I just hoped they'd move down to the woods this next week as I was sure I was already becoming far too attached to eat them.

All the sheep, except Apricot, were now sheared and much more comfortable. She was trimmed for sale but had too much wool on, so would hopefully be sheared that weekend. The ewe Aub and Tim brought in is also looking far happier out of her wool. She was quietly sheared standing up, but we still don't really know her problem. She has a normal temperature and is eating well, but her breathing continues to be more laboured than normal, so is still being treated with antibiotics. Tamsin will look at her next week when she comes to check the ewe with the broken leg, but her advice at the moment is just a broad-spectrum antibiotic.

Having removed the electric tape between the two ponies as they seemed to be getting on so well, Clemmie kicked her silver unicorn. I think she was cross that Sam hadn't turned them out promptly enough, so took it out on Dougal. Not life threatening, thank goodness. A sore muscle on his lower thigh, but quite unnecessary. The tape went back up.

Then a vet was needed as one of the white gimmers was found unable to use her back legs. Katy was the attending vet this time, who was quite hopeful of a successful outcome, feeling she may have twisted or knocked her back, rather than doing any permanent damage. She wasn't so confident about the other poorly ewe. Her breathing looked strained and Katy felt she may have some permanent lung damage, following pneumonia last winter. Oh the joys of sheep farming.

We moved the ewes and lambs out of the 18 acre over a week ago, to conform with our stewardship agreement, but there appeared to be at least five lambs happily grazing there this morning. As I walked down the 9 acre I was aware of several gaps in the fence. Obviously, we're still waiting for Dave.

Apricot was still not convinced she could survive

solely on grass although I've explained several times that most sheep can. She and her children were now moved onto Top Verandas, as grass was getting a little short in the 2 acre, so she had taken to galloping straight past Aub and the gator when he opened the gate, and with children in hot pursuit arrives in the yard looking for breakfast. She may soon realise that this isn't going to materialise and stay put in the field.

Yesterday when it was wet she looked so smug in her trimmed coat, lying under the trees with the others sheltering there. She will lose this as soon as the weather improves and it'll be interesting to see what's underneath.

Entire families now seemed to have moved back into the 18 acre. Quite amazing why they wanted to, as the grass is just as good in the 9 acre. Later that day Aub struggled up the field with a whole roll of wire, only to have me locate another hole near the top of the field, which we blocked with a hurdle. Then we chased all the families, there were now quite a few of them, back out of the field. Some were right at the top and it was hilarious to see them trying to locate their escape route to return through, but thwarted by the new wire. Eventually they accepted they'd have to go out of the gate.

The ewe with the broken leg was looking so much better. Tamsin took the bandage off and we left the ewe in the new shed to get used to the fact her leg didn't weigh quite as much. Unfortunately, Tamsin's prognosis not so good for the gimmer with the damaged back or the ewe breathing heavily so a decision had to be made on both.

Two of our Blue texel rams were selected to go on AHDB's Ram Compare programme, where different breeds are trialled to see which produce the best meat lambs from commercial ewes. We have sent rams before and they have given top class results, so very proud of them. We are waiting to see where and when they are going in the country. Our last two went to Northumberland so I was hoping we wouldn't have to transport these to the same farm. It was only a few days later that we were asked to do just that, but this would be the week after I had my knee operated on and I really didn't feel I'd cope with the journey.

On contacting Bridget at AHDB I suggested we could provide transport for the rams as far as Harrogate as a friend competing at the Great Yorkshire show had room in his trailer, so arrangements were made for another farmer who was also delivering sheep to Northumberland would meet and pick up the rams and take them on with his.

The weather was lovely. Clemmie seemed to have lost part of her mane, just noticed it; the children had probably used it as a handle when riding her.

The grass had really grown. We needed to sort out what we were cutting for hay, and topping the rest as the sheep end up with sore feet when the long grass runs through the cloves in their hooves. The last of the bottle lambs seemed content without bottles, now they had all finally been weaned. We moved some sheep from the 2 acre and pulled off a lamb not looking good and slipped him into the weaned lamb department.

Having kept the group with the new lamb in for three days, I discovered he'd gone missing in the evening. Eventually found him in the quarry field, probably looking for his mother, but she's not in that field. He'd gone right into the walk in creep and been trodden on by others. We rescued him and put him in with the smaller bottle lambs in the stable, making them stay in for a few days so we didn't have a repeat of his escape, but he seemed to settle in well.

Then we mislaid Chilli, Apricot's ram lamb. As the evening wore on, Aub and I both searched the field, the grass is very long on Top Veranders. Eventually I put Maisie round the sheep and Apricot found him hidden under a bush. Field needs topping.

Continuing the theme of twilight adventures, we had a pig-escape while Aub was topping up waters in the stable. Two piglets ran back in quite easily but a third made a dash for freedom through the gate into the back field of bottle lambs. All the livestock galloped round together, not helped by Jess joining in.

I cannot believe how good Sidney looks now. He's fleshed up like a proper lamb, or as a friend described him, not a tent anymore, more a fully-furnished yurt.

We backfat scanned the main lot of lambs, which gives us an indication of those with good muscle and fat cover. Those with the best results will stay on to be sold as shearling rams the following year. We couldn't do the whole flock as there were sheep in too many fields to get them all in. Aub had to move bags of wool I'd mentioned were in the way for some weeks, so was in a foul mood before we even got started. Stuart, our scanner, was using a new machine which took about three times as long as the old one, so it seemed like a long day.

The earlier lambs were weaned – moved onto fresh pasture without their mums so that the ewes could get a bit of peace. Jess proved what a super dog she is in the pens. Maisie is very cautious in a mob of sheep, not that I blame her, but Jess is totally fearless, which makes working in the handling unit so much easier.

The lambs went back in the 18 acre, and hopefully would stay there now the fence had been repaired. It's the field they're most likely to stay in while we're away at the weekend. The ewes went into the field opposite the sheep shed, which was sparse of grass now, thus easing milk production. There was very little shouting so I think they were relieved to part with their children. It's a bit like sending them off to school.

The bottle lambs sleep in two different places although all go out in the back field daily. Tonight they showed they were not well hefted to their departments. Several came in the wrong gate and spent most of the night complaining they were in the wrong bed. Interesting to see which gate they come in tomorrow.

First job this morning (which Aub had forgotten about) was to castrate a neighbour's goat kid. This proved more difficult than he'd anticipated, with the nanny taking off out of the pen, then running back in and knocking Aub's shin against a piece of metal. Very painful. He doesn't like goats anyway.

I was rushing round sorting out licenses and kit for us and the sheep to go away for three days to the Devon County Show. With lockdown it's been so long since we've done this that everything needs finding.

Kate trimmed the show sheep a few days ago. The two gimmers were wild and as strong as bulls so we'd attempt to halter train them like Aub used to with the Simmental bulls when he was working at Miserden. Instead of tying them to a tractor, we secured them to the back of the gator. The result was amazing. The two ewes had stood for over an hour on the trimming stand, and then spent a further hour the following day tied up in the shed and being handled. Now it was time to see if they would walk. One was quite cooperative but the other tried her hardest to refuse until Aub drove a bit faster and she had no choice but to follow.

Eventually they trotted along quite well, until Aub had to turn round. Ropes got tangled up and then disconnected. Abandoning the gator we each led a ewe back to the yard, gave her a cuddle and her tea and congratulated ourselves. It had been quite a result.

In the pig woodland at Bisley Lane Farm

Aub and the dogs moving the ewes

JULY

Men are definitely from Mars, women from Venus, or at least the way their brains work are as far apart as this. Who, in their right mind, decides to move sheep from one field to another, especially when they have to pass through another field of sheep, on the day we're driving to a show in Devon?

"Why do it today?" I asked

"Because they're out of grass."

"Couldn't you see that yesterday, or Tuesday?"

Tension was running high when Aub turned the ewes and lambs from the Quarry field into the field behind the buildings, which was also holding the ewes and lambs from Top Verandas. The Quarry field lot were supposed to turn right through the gateway and off to the Ruin. Of course they didn't. Aub had both dogs with him. I'd pushed the Top Verandas ewes tight to the buildings and all would have worked if the Quarry field lot had turned right. I jumped up and down and shouted, waving a large stick, but still they ignored me. They just ran straight towards the other sheep. Obviously, this was completely my fault.

We then had to run everything through the handling unit while I racked my brains to remember everyone who had been on Top Verandas. I'm not sure I got it totally right, but we ended up with some semblance of order.

I tried very hard to be calm. It wasn't going to improve matters if I said anything. And I mean anything! Just let's try to get the show on the road. Sarah, a friend from Devon had sent a text asking what time we were leaving. I'd said we'd aim for 11.30, so call that 12.30. It was now 1.15.

The trip to Devon was fairly uneventful. I exchanged texts with others on the M5 who were heading for the show and we eventually all met up at the showground around 5pm. Sheep unloaded, fed and watered, we checked in at our hotel, then back to the showground for a barbeque with most of the other Blue Texel competitors. A great evening, with more sausages, burgers and pork steaks than should have been eaten, plenty of drink and the grand finale of chocolate cookies and sweets. Giles embarrassed himself with a striptease, but we forgave him. The weather was warm till after ten, when we all felt we needed to go to bed, some camping and others, like us, heading for the hotel.

Show day and what a beautiful day. It started bright, promising to be very warm later, which it was. Our sheep looked a picture, but sadly not to the judge's taste. He liked the smaller, Beltex type. Ours are larger, stronger animals, so our two gimmers only managed third and fourth. At this point you remember sheep you've left in the field that might have suited the judge far better, however one of the ram lambs surprised us with a 2nd.

Everyone had some rosettes and we all had a great day, meeting up with friends we'd not seen for a long time. Congratulations to the show committee, who did so well to organise this within lockdown regulations. Numbers had been limited and the showground was big enough for everyone to give each other healthy space with everything happening in the fresh air. While Covid was still a consideration, the vaccination programme gave a certain sense of security, and good manners prevailed throughout. Avoiding the Friday evening traffic on the M5, along with Bec and Steve we stayed with Texel breeder friends in Dorset, Ian and Fiona, who gave us our wonderful lockdown puppy. Great to see Jess's mum and dad again. A fantastic stopover, lovely barbeque and brilliant group of friends.

All the fields needed topping. It's reminiscent of the lovely song 'Oh what a beautiful morning' where the grass is as high as an elephant's eye. The only trouble is that several of my Blue gimmers have cloudy eyes now, reacting to the long grass. Typically, when Tamsin came last week I didn't realise how low we were on Alamycin, which we use to treat this condition, so drove to the vet clinic at Quedgeley, half an hour away, to collect more. The most direct route is via Painswick, but the lanes are narrow and never straight. Usually this isn't a problem as most drivers know the area and drive accordingly. Not if you are a delivery driver and should be able to complete your parcel drops in a ridiculously short time.

The grey van appeared on a bend as if by magic. Knowing the road, I was going slowly and well into my side. Sadly the road wasn't really wide enough for both of us and he wasn't aiming to stop. Not sure if he simply couldn't or thought he could get through. As he clipped my wing mirror I braked and was almost stationary when there was a horrid tearing sound as he removed the back of my car. On inspection it appeared he'd taken the wheel arch and back bumper off.

He eventually stopped some way down the road. I did wonder if he was just going to carry on, but in all fairness the road was narrow there and I think he was just finding somewhere safer to park. When I asked him how much road he'd needed, he just said he'd got a big van! We exchanged details politely. (He was bigger than me!) Having discussed the situation with Aub on the phone, it was decided the garage was the best place to head for, and he'd come and collect me. I picked up some loose part of my injured car and put that on the back seat, hooked the disconnected bumper onto a more secure piece, then with hazard lights flashing drove slowly to Bisley. The right wing mirror refused to move back into position, making it more difficult to see if the bumper was staying on board, but I soon discovered the scuffing noise indicated when it wasn't. I only had to stop and re-adjust three times, before delivering it …

We had around 60 acres of grass to cut for hay, although some didn't get cut until the evening. Not ideal, as the sugars rise in the grass in the morning, making the crop more nutritional if it is cut earlier in the day, but being a small fish in a contactor pond we have to take it as we can. The weather was fantastic, or unbearably hot, depending on the individual; the long-range forecast a farmer's dream. I think every farmer and contractor in the country was either making hay or combining.

It turned out that what looked like fairly superficial damage to my lovely car resulted in the insurers writing it off. I was so fed up. It took me ages to find my lovely blue Subaru three years ago and it would probably take forever to find another car. As I wouldn't be driving for a while after my knee operation, I guess there was no rush and I should just be grateful I wasn't damaged.

The phone call asking if I was happy to have my knee replacement at the local Nuffield Hospital instead of Gloucester General, had come towards the end of our April lambing. Happy? I was delighted. I'd had my left knee replaced at the Winfield under our son Mark's Company insurance, but this second operation would be under the National Health, so a private room at the Nuffield with en suite was an unexpected luxury. Aub was horrified when I told him about the changed appointment – he thought I meant they wanted to admit me at that point, but I assured him we would have finished lambing before I went in.

My knee saga was a result, some sixteen years ago, of an overzealous ewe. Guarding her lambs, she charged at the sheepdog, who shot behind me for cover, resulting in the powerful impact of lowered skull hitting my left knee at considerable speed and strength, pushing my knee sideways.

My GP at the time was a top sports doctor, who arranged a physio package which had me walking again within two weeks, and kept the knee together for a further nine years, but eventually the pain became too much and I had the first operation.   I'm sure my right knee compensated for the left one, causing problems that had now come to light.

Regardless of my pain, my present GP simply recommended to 'keep taking the pills', so eventually I booked an appointment with one of the other practice doctors. She was horrified when she heard the creaking noises my knee made when bent. Fairly similar to an old wooden boat in a storm. The newspapers were full of reports about the awful backlog the NHS must have at this moment after all those cancelled operations, so I was amazed at the speed with which this all happened.

All these weeks later in July, after several visits, hours of form filling, swabs and Covid tests, I was admitted early Saturday morning to the Nuffield in Cheltenham. My first knee operation had coincided with Badminton horse trials weekend. This time I would to be able to watch both the lady's and men's final at Wimbledon and the England/Italy football final, should I wish to. After a spinal injection for pain relief and general anaesthetic, the next thing I remember was watching the final shots in the lady' singles final. It was good to have something take my mind off my knee. One of those situations, similar to childbirth, where you ask yourself 'why did I do that again?' and memories of the pain of the first incident come flooding back. This was exaggerated by lack of breath, a reaction to the general anaesthetic, so I was connected to oxygen for the next twenty-four hours, along with a hydrating drip.

After childbirth you think you've had all the embarrassments possible, but not so. Eventually I needed a wee. Balancing on a bedpan is certainly an acquired skill, one I might have mastered some years ago, but was struggling with at that moment. Assuring the nurse I could make it to the loo, she pointed to numerous pipes and machines I was attached to, which wouldn't come with me. Thankfully, later on the night nurse suggested using the commode, which rapidly advanced to walking to the adjacent bathroom, once I'd been helped out of the bed.

I eventually rang Aub about 7pm, knowing he'd be wondering how I was. I didn't have a lot to relay, but asked how his day had gone. Overjoyed that the hay was cut and the long range forecast good, that afternoon he'd dropped the two Blue Texel rams with Trevor in Oxfordshire, to travel to Harrogate on Sunday. Then he admitted he'd had an accident with the gator, (farm truck). In one of our steepest fields, he'd spied a lamb with a problem. Getting out to check it, he was suddenly aware the gator was moving past him, with both dogs still on board. Managing to run alongside, he'd scrambled in, slamming the brake on hard; which spun the vehicle round to a very unstable position. Then, with sufficient throttle power, he forced it forward and safely manoeuvred up the hill again. I was horrified.

After a further cocktail of pain relief, I sent Aub a text saying how much I appreciated him rescuing the dogs and stopping the gator, but he was even more important than Maisie and Jess, and please would he not kill himself while I was in hospital. Then to sleep before the painkillers wore off.

The lovely night nurse told me I must keep the operated leg straight. Little good telling that to someone who turns over around 26 times during the night, spending half the night sleeping on her stomach, but pain did direct me to a correct position. Complaining sufficiently, I was dosed with liquid morphine between other pain relief. At the mention of morphine, I imagined I would be totally out of it, but unfortunately the dose was very low, although I did manage to sleep until the next pill run.

There was no subtle dawn chorus in Cheltenham. Close to the Severn estuary, the gulls argued all night, and as day broke, their calls became even more dominant and echoed over greater distances. There may be other birds celebrating the new day, but their songs are drowned by herring gull's laughter.

My leg was so painful over the next two days. The nurses removed the massive bandage and changed the dressing underneath on the second day, before physio and more torture. I don't remember being in so much pain last time, but perhaps we just forget. Still, that was seven years ago, I've got a bit more decrepit since then.

I was meant to be going home on the third day, so alerted Aub to fit in picking me up around eleven. Slightly worried that I hadn't practiced on stairs yet, but expected it would go OK. Pain improving slightly but just sensible to take pills half an hour before physio.

Everything was late, including Aub. who arrived at 12.30pm having had to collect some brackets for some hay related machinery. Then some complication with my medication was going to hold things up for another thirty minutes, so I suggested Aub popped to Asda next door and picked up some sandwiches for lunch. Having rung the buzzer to attract the nurse to sort out my pills, I then realised part of the paperwork she was looking for was on one of the tables, so pressed the buzzer again, unaware she hadn't switched it off on her first visit. Alarms rang all over the building, and within seconds I had about seven nursing staff arrive at the door.

Horrified, I burst out laughing, saying I now knew how to attract their attention. The paperwork and tablets were sorted rapidly so I rang Aub back to tell him. He was in B&Q car park, looking for Asda. (B & Q is the opposite side of the hospital to Asda.) It must be a man thing. I suggested he came back and picked me up and I'd sort lunch when we got home.

Aub's real worry was still the hay. The contractor cuts and bales, but Aub turns it to keep the costs down a bit, and everything seems to work smoothly. Although not always. We bought a 'new' turner two years ago, and in all fairness it is only used for haymaking, but sods law a tyre had split, holding things up while another was ordered. Luckily the tyre man was going to a neighbouring farm so put a new tyre on for us and all was up and running again that afternoon.

Everyone was at it. Tractors, trailers and combines were driving past the house at regular intervals, from mid-morning until late evening; all in a rush to be somewhere else.

On our own fields, all the grass was now turned, some of it twice. The sun was hot and with a slight breeze all looked able to be baled for hay, saving on the costs of wrapper (turning it into haylage) and more diesel which was great.

I, of course, saw very little of this. I was beginning to get fed up with 'Homes under the Hammer' and 'Bargain Hunt'. I did have quite a good book on the go, and was writing when I could, but it was not the most comfortable position for my leg under my desk. Walking round the house and doing an array of exercises added variation but not much by the way of scenery. Walking outside was limited as the yard was so uneven.

Every five to six hours I studied the cocktail of pills, making sure I'd taken one of each at the required time. Quite testing. When you come out of hospital you are issued with all of these, but not with a timetable, and I vaguely remember being told to take one lot separate from the codeine and paracetamol, but what the heck. As long as I don't overdose on anything I'm sure it will all work out.

Every Saturday morning from about May this year Kate has run a stand at the local Farm Shop selling Bisley Lane Free Range Pork and Bacon and Shorthorn Beef, and it's going incredibly well. Now set up with a new chiller cabinet the display looks appealing and sales are buoyant. Free Range lamb should be adding to their stock in a couple of weeks.

On the hay side of things, everything was baled. Now to get it all in. I didn't dare ask if Aub had a plan, as he rarely does, but the weather was still very much on our side.

At my first check-up at the hospital with the physio, I thought I was getting on quite well, but physio chap was not quite as impressed as I thought he should be. I made sure I'd taken a top up of pills before I saw him, but my leg was still painful after I was drilled to do squats and leg raising to a higher degree than I'd been doing. Home for ice packs, a rest and 'Escape to the Country'!

Mark's birthday and Dave the fencing man was available. Hopefully he would get Mark's gateposts at the entrance to Bisley Lane Farm in and hang the gates; this was his requested birthday present. Unfortunately for Mark, it turned out that it was in fact the same request he'd made last year. I'd been unaware of this, and as Dave had never been available, it still hadn't been done. While I try hard not to shout and interfere with things I cannot assist with myself, I had rung Dave this time to ensure he appeared. As far as presents go, we farmers really know how to treat ourselves.

I was doing the sale entries for the pedigree sheep without physically seeing the animals, which was proving difficult. I just hoped I could substitute some if my original choices don't prove right. While I hadn't progressed to the farm yet, dog walking – with a stick as the ground is very undulated – is now a regular occurrence. Otherwise they'd spend all day in their kennel.

Most of the hay was now under cover. Still a few out, which was a little worrying, but nothing I could say or do about it. The forecast was for the weather to break at any moment.

It was delivery day to Julian's farm, where 115 big bales had been sold off the field. Dave (the illusive Dave) and Wilf, who we've known since we lived in Througham, were helping with their own tractors and trailers. Aub was driving the JCB as this was needed to unload at Julian's.

Julian's farm has the most awkward access possible. The land slopes, though the barns for storing the hay are on adjacent land with less undulations. Access with a tractor and trailer is from the main Stroud road, then everyone parks up while Aub unloads and stacks the barns. Apparently, all was going well, with Aub unloading the back two bales from Wilf's trailer. This team have been doing this for several years now, the procedure being that once the eight back bales were unloaded, the trailer was reversed back to enable Aub to collect the next bales. As he backed out of the barn to fetch the second lot, Aub was horrified to see two bales on the ground, where Wilf had been standing.

Realising Wilf was under the bales, Aub lifted both off him as quickly as possible, then secured the trailer with the JCB, ensuring nothing else could fall. It appeared that when Wilf had undone the second lot of straps the bales had fallen off. By now Andy, Julian's shepherd was phoning for an ambulance.

Wilf was not in a good way, although the fact that both bales had fallen did mean one had broken the fall of the other, and their full weight had fallen either side of him, rather than one crushing him. The men made him as comfortable as possible while waiting for emergency services. Andy was still on the phone being told ambulances would have to come from Bristol. Obviously, the exchange had no idea of the severity of the accident or the time it would take an ambulance to get up the M5 from Bristol to Stroud on a Friday afternoon, so Aub insisted they needed the air ambulance. This was confirmed. Wilf's family were contacted and soon arrived.

Then the fiasco began. I can only relay what Aub and the others told me. Firstly a fire engine arrived, luckily coming into the field the same way as the tractors, followed by two small ambulances. Next the air ambulance managed to land, although the fields are not ideal for that. The paramedics on board were the life savers, treating Wilf immediately, with pain relief and immobilising him, and soon he was unaware of much. Then the pilot discovered they had an oil leak on both engines, so would not be able to transport him to Southmead, where he was destined.

Neither of the road ambulances were mechanically up to the trip to Bristol, so a further call was made for a larger ambulance, which decided it couldn't come into the field, but parked at the pub at the top of the hill. Having topped poor Wilf up with morphine and secured him in a stretcher the only solution appeared to put him on the back of the farm gator and drive up the narrow road to the pub, where he was transferred to the waiting ambulance and began his journey to Bristol.

It sounded an absolute nightmare. Thankfully the air ambulance paramedics, although unable to transport Wilf, did ensure his wellbeing on site, and administered strong pain relief. While his injuries were extreme, a fractured pelvis, damaged spine and broken ankle as far as we were able to gauge at that point, had they been any more life threatening it's frightening to think of the outcome, with all the delays involved in transporting him to hospital.

Gradually the ambulances and fire crew dispersed, the air ambulance able to travel back to Bristol, but not considered safe enough to carry a patient! Although both still in a state of shock, Aub and Dave continued to unload the trailers, then drove back to Edgeworth to bring in the final forty bales still in the field, as the forecast was for torrential rain that night. That's farmers for you.

We were so relieved to hear that Wilf was in a stable condition, however, they weren't planning to operate until Monday. Then there were more delays on Wilf's operations due to a possible blood clot, but Aub chatted to him by phone and he seemed relatively comfortable, if that's possible.

The poor man ended up having his right ankle

operated on. He also had his pelvis pinned, suffered three damaged vertebrae and seven broken ribs. I don't think he'll be rushing around for a while yet. I spoke with him and we exchanged pain, although I feel my knee is less than his problems.

Haymaking

Kate selling at the farm shop

AUGUST

The phone was ringing with ram buyers. For the past two weeks, all had been quiet during the endless sunshine, every farmer in the country either haymaking or harvesting, but now they had time to think about breeding stock and the start of another year.

The weather had changed completely, the temperature dropped and the days grey and cloudy. When Aub called the lambs in this evening, he realised 'Baby' wasn't with the others, so searched in the back field only to find her dead under the trailer. She'd seemed perfectly healthy, skipping out with the others that morning as usual. Having kept her going from a tiny lamb for the past three months we were both gutted. The trouble is you never know if they've had sufficient colostrum from the ewe and although I know she had artificial also, that may have proved insufficient in the end. She'd always been very small, not growing on as well as I expected her to, although having all the food and facilities she needed so perhaps there was something deep down that wasn't right. We can't save them all, but it still makes me sad.

I did wonder if we should have entered the early ram sale at Builth, but buyers started to arrive on farm and by the end of this week we had sold twelve, so our decision to stay at home was the best. Some just came to select, not wanting them yet, while others took their rams away. Several pedigree Blue Texel buyers came looking for good shearling rams and three now went to new homes.

Fed up that I was still unable to go to the farm, I foolishly checked in to another online sheep sale, this time in Ireland, where our friends Janet and Andy were selling some more lovely Blue Texels. There were two really nice ewe lambs I liked, and Aub even agreed, setting me a price limit though.

I managed to buy one, the other going quite a way above my limit, but Janet then offered me another she had at home, as we both thought the trip over here would be better if there were two together. Janet then asked me to send her pictures of our best ewes, saying she would be interested in something with good face markings, dark coat and big backside. The best I had to offer that fulfilled all those requirements was the ewe we'd taken third prize with at Devon. After negotiation she was sold to Janet. Now the only consideration was collecting my two lambs and sending Miserden Ember to Northern Ireland.

On Mark's farm, almost 100 acres of wild flowers and clover mix were being cut for haylage. As always it was down to Aub to turn the grass but it wasn't worth him going yesterday as the weather was so grey, but brightened up a bit this afternoon so all action. Some sunshine would be good.

On that score, we had the excellent news that Wilf was recovering well from his accident with the bales and should be fully mobile soon.

Friday 13th was not a good date, but a busy day. Aub and Mark did a pig run to the abattoir, before we took three Texel rams to Cirencester market, where Aub was inspecting the other stock at the Gloucester Texel Club sale. (Another breeder inspects ours.) A good crowd there and the rams sold quite well.

Jenny, who bought two homebred horses – daughters of our wonderful Dash – from me in the past, lives in Leicestershire, but she and some friends were staying fairly close by with their horses on a riding holiday, so I persuaded Aub to drive me over to see them, as I was still unable to drive. Solitaire, the first Jenny had from me was now in foal, having damaged herself eventing, but she was happily competing Royal.

When I arrived, Royal was in the paddock. I called to her and was thrilled when she lifted her head and whinnied back at me. It was four years since she'd last seen me. Jenny and I had a good catch up, followed by supper with friends at a local pub. We got home to find that Mark's haylage had been baled during the afternoon once the sun had crisped it up a bit more. Now there was just the job of bringing in about 800 bales!

With Aub all set to travel the length and breadth of the country inspecting white Texels later in the month, I was already planning to go with Giles and family to Carlisle for the Blue Texel sale, so plans evolved for transporting Ember to NI. Now NI is still part of the EU and we are not, there is far more paperwork involved in the journey, but hopefully all would fall into place. Blood samples were taken, Export Health Certificates issued and all looking good.

With the combination of sales and breeding plans, dates in August and September have to be worked out with military precision. Synchronised ewes come in to season together, in blocks of two or three lots and moving rams around means I have to study the calendar every morning religiously to know where I'm going and what I'm doing. Amazingly it generally works out OK.

Toby and Wilfred had a farming day helping us wean the later lambs, one operating the gate letting them out while the other sprayed a red line down the backs of the ewes to be sold. These older ewes deserve an autumn of good grass, some even having hard food if their teeth are lacking, to be culled before the winter.

Those still fit and healthy for lambing will also be put on good grazing, ready to go to the rams next month.

Toby found his ewe, Mittens and her two lambs. She was a more troublesome gift than we'd expected as she'd been pretty useless at looking after her lambs, not having proven to be a natural mother, but let's hope she improves next year. In some ways, the experience was more useful for Toby than if she'd been perfect. Toby decided that he'd like to have her at Bisley Lane farm, where he could see her and feed her daily to make her friendly. She could go there with Mark's Blue Texels once they were all in lamb. We told Toby we'd keep the lambs here so we could feed them up a bit and hopefully they should look viable later in the year.

Both boys seemed to enjoy their day, having a great time guiding the sheep back to their relevant fields, one on the quad, the other driving the buggy under grandpa's supervision, each with a sheepdog alongside.

In fact, they must have enjoyed themselves because they both came back for another day farming. While we expected Toby, who had camped the previous night with a friend, to be sleepy, it was Wilfred who wilted a bit in the sun before lunch. Revived for the afternoon both boys helped to push lambs forward, while we sorted the ram lambs from the ewe lambs, reading the weights of those ready to go for meat along with operating the weighing machine gates. Happy but tired they both left with their well-earned payments in their hands.

A week of chaos began. Firstly, just to add to the mix a man from Defra rang up and wanted to do a sheep check tomorrow. I assured him he couldn't, but he still wanted to check up on the movements and paperwork. Luckily, it was fairly up together so I agree to that, but bringing in 60 lambs for him to check ear tags would have to wait until next week.

The bottle lambs needed worming and fly repellent, which took far longer than it should have done because moving bottle lambs is much like herding cats. No one wants to go a new and different way from the route they usually take, they totally ignore the dogs, or embarrass them by kissing them, and tempers were slightly frayed. Some shearling ewes had to be taken to Giles's farm near Ledbury, meat lambs sorted for a six am delivery to the abattoir tomorrow morning and a slow puncture grounded the gator.

After dropping off the ewes, we drove to the site of the old Gloucester market, now a busy shopping and fast-food mall, and dined on McDonalds as I didn't know when I'd fit in cooking supper. The chips were good but the burger and bun were pretty revolting. Almost like varying layers of cardboard but it filled a gap. Sitting in the car eating our supper I saw that Domino's pizza place was open till 5am, and we were reminded of late nights at Ken's Chinese back when the market site was still a cattle market, a million years ago.

It was ten o'clock before we managed to round

up the lambs and secure them in the shed, the dogs working brilliantly in the dark, then a further half hour before Aub eventually found and repaired the puncture.

Believe it or not, it was lovely to hear birdsong at 5.30 this morning. I hadn't been awake at this time for a few weeks, but we needed to be back from the abattoir by seven for Aub to leave for Birmingham airport at eight to fly to Edinburgh. Mark T in charge of feeding, and although I still had things to do while Aub was away it felt somewhat of a relief when he left. Stress levels definitely diluted. After an hour with the 'man from the ministry' all looked good, with the promise of a return visit Thursday week, once we were both back from sales.

Aub arrived back from Lanark a few days later, late at night, then he delivered me to G's early this morning for a horrendous eight hour trip to Carlisle with our Blue Texels while he had an equally stressful trip to Welshpool. I'd hoped to see the Badgerface sale during the afternoon but it was almost over by the time we arrived, the M6 having been a nightmare.

We were just in time for the Blue Texel show, prior to tomorrow's sale, and I took my best gimmer in. She made the front line but not the rosettes, but it was amazing how many people saw and admired her there.

The sale turned into a depressingly long wait while around 300 rams went through the ring. Several shearlings and a few ram lambs made good money but there were so many embryo transfer lambs of the same or similar breeding that buyers lost interest. During the waiting period I collected the two ewe lambs that had travelled from Northern Ireland, and purchased a Badgerface shearling ram, although forbidden to do so by Aub. Not the biggest, but a very correct sheep which hadn't made his reserve the previous day.

It was almost four thirty before the females sold, but luckily some buyers were still there and both ours and Giles's gimmers sold well. We gathered ourselves up for the return trip, leaving Carlisle at teatime and arriving home after midnight. It was a very long two days, but wonderful for my knee which benefitted from the miles I must have walked on concrete over the two days – or at least so I told myself.

August really is the month of sales. Our next stop was the English Texel sale at Worcester. Another hard day inspecting for Aub, but I stayed in bed at the hotel, had a long shower and lazy breakfast before joining him at lunchtime! Might as well spoil myself. Two white texel ram lambs were purchased to add to the team, one in half share with another local breeder.

It feels like a familiar pattern now. And so on to the farming year's end, and the beginning of September.

The Blue Texel sale at Worcester, with neither the quality or the money changing hands as it had at

Carlisle. One of our gimmers sold through the ring, but I was disappointed that my best one failed to make her reserve. Someone did make a low offer for her outside the ring, which I politely refused, then a well-known breeder bought her for her full value so a successful day after all.

Moreton in Marsh Show was the season's finale. Aub's lovely Texel ewe cut her eye so didn't go, which was probably a good job as he had the job of showing my Blue gimmer which proved a bit of a handful in the ring. It was sad that Giles failed to capture on camera some of their antics, but Aub eventually contained her enthusiasm to win her class and become Reserve Breed Champion.

An excellent finish to a somewhat limited show season.

Aub guided my Blue gimmer to win
Reserve Breed Champion

THE VIEW AHEAD

Our Blue Texels were a storming success earlier this year, and later sales both at home and in the markets have been great. The rest of this month looks as full as always, breeding plans well underway for Texels, Blue Texels and now Badgerface Texels, the breeding and sales season being the start and finale of our farming year. Although we sold several really good shearling ewes, I've retained ten of our best Blue Texels as breeding stock, and spend hours gazing at them as they graze on Verandas.

Autumn is such a lovely time on the farm. Mornings when the sun gradually breaks through the mist, opening up an ethereal vista of greens and yellows, turning to golds. The moisture clings to the Blue Texels, coating them in silver. Blackberries are profuse, their scent almost as good as their taste. But it's a time of reflection as well as looking forward. What worked well this year, and what should we do to improve things for next?

The rams will definitely come out from the ewes on time and lambing won't be so prolonged. Saying that, we have decided the commercial sheep are little bother to lamb in April, so a second lambing, which Aub swore we wouldn't do again, will still happen. But the rams WILL come out after two weeks. No more June lambs.

The response we have all had to our locally produced meat has been exceptional and we must continue to produce the lamb alongside Kate and Mark's beef and pork. While the past twelve months has brought concern to many, it has also made people think more about the quality of their lives and in many ways their food standards.

The shows will be back next year, the social interaction that is so important to all our lives will once again return. Aub and I have already accepted invitations to judge in May, and are sure to exhibit our own stock during the summer.

There's the progress of Bisley Lane Farm and our four enthusiastic young farmers to look forward to. Dates have already been booked by the boys for farming days, and I'm sure Bluebell will want to be involved as well. They even have friends who are desperate to come for night lambing shifts. I'm not sure if Aub is quite prepared for this. Maybe we'll have to do an open day for parents to bring their children along for a lambing experience.

There are unexpected gains too – as I write this, Toby has just started at secondary school and rugby has turned out to be his greatest love. I suppose wrestling matches with young pigs are just another form of training.

While the woods are full of black spotted pink piglets, the roar of fallow bucks can also be heard. Venison may be on the menu by Christmas.

Walking through the fields together, just before dusk, both dogs containing their energy and walking to heel, it's great to lean against a hayrack with Aub and just absorb the atmosphere. From top verandas we can see if all is well, the mist forming again in ribbons across the valley. Apricot will usually find us and search for titbits, often unsuccessfully. Lights from the neighbouring farm remind us there are many others checking their stock as well. These are the moments you need to hold on to and remember.

Acknowledgements

A big thank you to Aub for checking and feeding on cold winter evenings while I've sat in my office writing, with the heating on! To our children, their partners and our grandchildren for making events happen and their continued interest in this mad farming life. To Mary Griese for reading sentences I couldn't get right, and aligning them perfectly. To Lorna of Crumps Barn Studio for making it happen, as always, and designing a particularly lovely cover.

And finally a big Thank You to all our farming friends worldwide, who appear to have read and enjoyed the previous books. Your accolades have been a terrific boost.

About the author

Sue Andrews is a journalist and sheep farmer. She has written for county magazines and the national equestrian and farming press. She and her husband Aubrey are established breeders of both Texel and Blue Texel sheep. Their close involvement with the work of both Breed Societies has taken them all over Europe. Their prize-winning Miserden Texel sheep have been successfully exhibited at major shows up and down the country. This is her third book about life on their busy Cotswold sheep farm.

It seems an impossible dream at first for Sue and Aubrey.
She is a horse-mad girl strongly attracted to the idea of farming,
Aubrey is the son of a farm manager without land or money.
But with limited knowledge, much enthusiasm and the
challenge of raising their young family, anything can happen.

Turn the page for an exclusive extract

**This is where the story begins:
a true story of the shepherding life –
amusing, poignant and beautifully detailed …**

Exclusive Extract from
If Clouds Were Sheep

In the Beginning

W as it faith in ourselves or a flight of fancy that allowed us to dream of farming? We had no inherited farm, no livestock and very little money. My dream included horses. For Aubrey, farming was in his blood.

As a farm manager with no family farm to pass on, his father encouraged both his sons towards different careers. Aub qualified as an agricultural engineer, but his determination to farm never faltered, and in no time I was swept along on the same wave.

As a child I gazed longingly at the thoroughbred mares and foals grazing at the Jevington Stud on the South Downs, while Aubrey spent his holidays gathering sheep on the fells with his younger brother John, their uncle, cousins and local farmers and sons.

Family holidays were mainly spent on his aunt and uncle's farm near Kirkby Lonsdale, where they ran Dalesbred and Swaledale sheep. The promise of a warm sunny day, ideal for collecting for shearing, heralded an early start. The old Land Rover took them part way up the fell, but there was always at least another hour of upward trek before they started the descent, bringing the flock in.

Aubrey loved the sounds of the fells. The bleating of sheep, music from skylarks and the occasional mew of a buzzard, although that could herald a death. The breeze, however warm there was always a breeze. The dogs were magic. While occasional whistles were heard on the wind, the dogs worked from instinct and knowledge rather than instructions.

The raucous baas as ewes called lambs to stay close. This mob increased as ewes and lambs from further outlying runs joined the main flock heading down the valley, where they were sorted into those owned by his uncle and those of other farmers. His uncle's ewes had a blue paint mark on their left shoulder, while neighbouring farmers' stock may have a red mark in the same position or blue on the right shoulder, or black on the quarter; whatever colour and position they've used on that holding for centuries.

The rough grazing and craggy outcrops gently blended with a softer landscape as they neared the valley. At some point during the gather there would be time for the boys to stop and lie back on the course brittle grass to recover. His aunt would have sent him off with sandwiches and cake as would the other mothers.

They would scoop clear sparkling water into their hands from the small springs that appeared at intervals throughout the hills. Camaraderie was great but it was also fun to be on his own, with Moss, his uncle's older dog, at his side. He would tire more quickly than the younger dogs and be happy to walk alongside Aubrey as he wound his way down into the valley. Here Aubrey was master of the fell, flockmaster and sheepdog handler. On a warm summer day he rarely ceased smiling.

The sheep would gradually slow their pace, eventually running through a narrow sorting race, lined with high stone walls so none could escape, where they were divided into the separate flocks. It takes a smart man with a quick eye to work the shedding gate which turns the sheep to left or right depending on flock mark which has often faded. All ewes and most of the lambs will have been marked before turning on the hill after lambing, but occasionally an unmarked lamb, born on the fell, will come through and need sorting once it goes to its mother.

Next day's clipping was even more exhausting. First the ewes were run into the clipping shed while the lambs ran back into a field. The noise was unbelievable as lambs were separated from their mothers, but they soon settled down to graze. The ewes were caught from a pen, turned by twisting their neck to overbalance them, then set on their backside. They usually sat in this position quite happily as the shearer reached up, pulled the string to start the machine and removed their fleece.

The belly was clipped first, then the wool on the back leg opened out to the tail. Blades were thrust in long confident strokes against the sheep's skin. Each sweep of their shears took a full comb of wool from the body, while keeping the fleece as one whole piece.

Aubrey was entranced by the shearers. It took minutes or less to shear a hill ewe, then they were re-marked with their farm's smit mark and turned back to their lambs with little or no stress. Before his uncle, or whoever he was helping, brought the next ewe out of the pen, it was Aubrey's job to gather up the fleece thrown to one side of the clipping board; roll it into a ball, stretching and twisting the neck into a rope to secure the fleece as his uncle had shown him. He then threw it into the wool sacks, later climbing in and trampling down the fleeces so more could be packed in a bag. He had to be quick. No one would wait for him to falter; for fear of back strain no shearer wants to stand upright between sheep.

The sounds of ewes calling to lambs and lambs calling back echoed across the valley. Eventually the motors would stop running and a picnic to surpass all others he'd ever seen was laid out in the barn on long trestle tables. Young boys could be clipped around the ear for sneaking a sausage roll in front of their seniors, but there was always plenty for everyone, washed down with endless mugs of tea. Aubrey often wondered how the shearers could bend over after such a lunch.

Later that summer both ewes and lambs would again be run through the stone lined race, this time into the deep circular trough used to dip them. He was again able to help with bringing the sheep off the fell and into the race, but his elders took over the dipping, plunging them into a foul-smelling grey liquid that would kill all the parasites the sheep were now carrying during the warm summer months. As they swam round looking for a way out, his uncle would poke them with a long metal pole, submerging them for longer than Aubrey thought was possible for them to hold their breath. Then to his relief they would clamber out of the dip and shake the excess off their wool.

"'As to be done lad, or they'd be eaten alive with maggots," he explained when Aubrey asked some of his many questions. "Flies lay eggs on their fleeces, especially the dirty bits round their back ends and when they hatch, them maggots live on sheep flesh if we don't do this to 'em."

One April, his uncle was ill at the start of lambing. Nearly fourteen, his mother agreed he could take the train to Kirkby Lonsdale and help his aunt and his young cousin with the lambing. Although others from neighbouring farms were taking turns helping out, it was a sharp learning curve for Aubrey. He walked for days on the in-bye fields checking that ewes and lambs were matched up and feeding well, his faithful friend Moss with him. Jack, from Far Fell, taught him to catch a ewe with a crook and tip her up so he could hold a daft lamb onto her teat to suckle. Once its stomach was full of milk it was content and seeing Moss lying down close by brought on a protective mothering ability to the young ewe.

"She'll sort it now," Jack told him as they moved on round the lambing fields to see what else needed assistance. Two weeks later, tired but incredibly happy he climbed on the train home assuring his aunt that he'd had the best Easter holiday possible.

The gripping second book in the series:

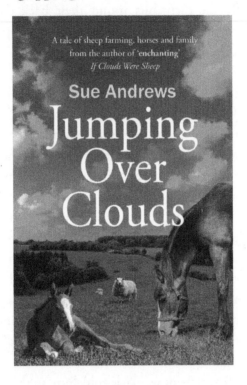

A tale of sheep farming, horses and family
from the author of 'enchanting'
If Clouds Were Sheep

Sue Andrews

Jumping Over Clouds

Young mum and shepherdess Sue Andrews is working hard to
make ends meet while she and husband Aubrey raise two small
children on their busy farm. They have a growing reputation for
breeding pedigree Texel sheep, but Sue also has a dream of her
own. She longs to breed and produce sports horses.

Jumping Over Clouds

**Humorous and beautifully captivating, this
is the true story of family life and horses on a
busy Texel sheep farm**